BREAD FOR THE WORLD

Bread for the World

by
Arthur Simon
Executive Director of
Bread for the World

PAULIST PRESS
New York / Paramus / Toronto
and
WM. B. EERDMANS PUBLISHING CO.
Grand Rapids

Library of Congress
Catalog Card Number: 75-16672

ISBN: 0-8091-1889-0

Published by Paulist Press
Editorial Office: 1865 Broadway, N.Y., N.Y. 10023
Business Office: 400 Sette Drive, Paramus, N.J. 07652

and
Wm. B. Eerdmans Publishing Co.
255 Jefferson S.E.
Grand Rapids, Mich. 49502

Printed and bound in the
United States of America

To Peter and Nathan

Contents

PART IV: A PROGRAM FOR ACTION

Preface

Although this book serves as a general introduction to world hunger, it emphasizes primarily the neglected role of public policy. Millions suddenly want to do something about world hunger. Few bother with public policy. Yet government policies may multiply or nullify a hundredfold all private efforts to assist hungry people. Ordinary persons can help to shape those policies. That is the thesis of this book. Because Christians have a special invitation to care about hungry people, the book is addressed primarily to them, but it is intended also for others.

The United States has steadily retreated from policies that would help hungry people. Much misunderstanding about hunger and its causes—and about what this country is doing—lies behind our retreat. A better understanding would go a long way toward helping the nation reach out to others in a manner worthy of its founding ideals.

Basic elements of a global plan to reduce hunger emerged at the World Food Conference in November 1974. The Conference named increased food production among the rural poor in Asia, Africa and Latin America as the primary strategy. How will that happen? This "simple" step requires that most nations, especially our own, put it high on their agendas when policies are developed and legislation is hammered out. To date neither Congress nor the Administration seems especially interested. But if alert voters in each congressional district began to insist, our leaders would soon respond.

I try to present this point of view without dwelling at length on aspects of hunger that are covered well in other books. A few of these, along with other resources, are listed in Chapter 14.

This book spells out some of the main themes that concern Bread for the World, a new Christian citizens' movement from which the book's title is taken. Although I wrote at the request of Bread for the World's Board of Directors (who are listed in the appendix), this book does not represent an official statement of policy. For that, the reader can check the appendix. Even there, Bread for the World's policy statement is a provisional draft submitted to the membership for review. I have tried to reflect the positions outlined in that statement, but because no two persons will do that in exactly the same way, each reader can make his or her own comparison.

Although this is a new book, it represents in part a revision of *The Politics of World Hunger* (Harper's Magazine Press, 1973) which I wrote with my brother Paul, now a member of Congress from Southern Illinois. Readers of both books will see similarities. Some of the themes in this one are discussed more fully in the earlier work, so it may have value as a further reference despite publication before the oil crisis.

I am indebted to those who read all or parts of this manuscript and offered helpful suggestions: Eugene Carson Blake, William J. Byron, C. Dean Freudenberger, Iqbal Haji, Hulbert H. James, Richard J. Neuhaus, Paul Simon, and my wife Kaiya. Stephen Coats, Barbara Howell, Brennon Jones and Carla Wharton did indispensable work in tracking down numerous statistics for me. All staff members of Bread for the World helped in various ways, taking on additional work so that I could write, and I am grateful to each of them. My family deserves a special word of appreciation for virtually losing a member of the family while this book was in process. None of the above deserves blame for the shortcomings of this book. All deserve thanks.

Arthur Simon
May 1975

Part I
The Struggle for Bread

1
Hunger

Hunger is a child with shrivelled limbs and a swollen belly.

It is the grief of parents, or a person gone blind for lack of vitamin A.

A single example of hunger is one too many. But in 1974 the United Nations reported that by the most conservative estimate, more than 460 million people are permanently hungry. They don't get enough calories to make a normal life possible and their number is increasing.

Without enough calories the body slows down and at some point starts to devour its own vital proteins for energy. When that happens, starvation has begun, a process described by *Time* this way:

> The victim of starvation burns up his own body fats, muscles and tissues for fuel. His body quite literally consumes itself and deteriorates rapidly. The kidneys, liver and endocrine system often cease to function properly. A shortage of carbohydrates, which play a vital role in brain chemistry, affects the mind. Lassitude and confusion set in, so that starvation victims often seem unaware of their plight. The body's defenses drop; disease kills most famine victims before they have time to starve to death. An individual begins to starve when he has lost about a third of his normal body weight. Once this loss exceeds 40 per cent, death is almost inevitable.[1]

460 million people are victims of acute hunger. If we widen the definition of hunger to include those who get enough calories, but not enough proteins or other essential nutrients and so can-

not function at full capacity, then the number of hungry people might reach anywhere from one to two billion, according to various estimates of the UN Food and Agriculture Organization.

Almost half of these people are young children.

When famine reaches dramatic proportions, we occasionally view on television the faces of hunger in refugee camps, shanty towns or crowded city streets. But for the most part hunger is invisible. Relatively few victims have shrivelled limbs or beg from tourists. Instead they suffer for years in quiet obscurity. Their bodies and often their minds function at half pace. They get sick too often and die too soon. When death arrives, it seldom comes as an undisguised case of starvation. Usually it takes the more merciful form of measles or diarrhea or some other ordinary disease.

In *Living Poor* Moritz Thomsen, a 48-year-old farmer from the state of Washington, tells of his experience as a Peace Corps volunteer in a remote village of Ecuador. During a drought people in a nearby village "were selling their children before they died of hunger; autopsies on the ones who had died revealed stomachs full of roots and dirt." In his own village, the birth of a stillborn child was occasion for jubilant celebration, since it meant that someone had become an *angelito* without all the suffering.

Thomsen, who paid a village family to let him eat his evening meal with them, describes the pathetic sight of their baby girl, malnourished and sickly, sleeping on the floor during mealtimes, or eating bits of banana or rice off the floor. He received favored treatment as a paying guest, but even that skimpy fare became more meager:

> Instead of fish and rice, we were tucking away *aba* soup, and rice with *abas*; *abas* being a large, fat, tasteless bean about 200 percent blander than a lima bean. The evening meal became more and more spiritual. A dozen or so times I staggered over to Alexandro's house, ravenous with hunger and anticipation, to find that supper was one well-centered and naked fried egg cowering on the plate. What made even this more or less tasteless was my knowledge that it was the only egg in the house and that the rest of the

family was supping on cups of hot water and brown sugar and platano, an enormous, banana-like monstrosity, about 99 percent starch, which was as tasteless as paper. Eating the only egg in the house while the youngest child slowly wasted away from malnutrition didn't help things either.[2]

Thomsen was initially outraged by the apparent laziness of the villagers—until circumstances forced him to eat what they ate. Then he discovered why many of the world's farmers are able to work only three or four hours a day. "There are just so many miles to a gallon of bananas," he observes.

Behind the overpowering, impersonal statistics on hunger are people, real people, suffering and dying because they do not enjoy a basic right that the rest of us take for granted: the right to a nutritionally adequate diet. And these individuals comprise much of the human family.

A New Focus on Hunger

Hunger is nothing new. Hunger drove the sons of Jacob to Egypt, where "the whole world came to buy corn from Joseph, so severe was the famine everywhere." Famines have occurred throughout history, some of them worse than those of the early and mid 1970s. Yet in the 1970s the world began paying far more attention to hunger. Three reasons account for this:

1. *Although famines have been just as severe before, the famines of the 1970s have been more widespread.* Hunger is increasingly determined by degree of poverty rather than by geography. Famine formerly struck isolated areas; but in the 1970s it touched Asia, Africa and to a lesser extent Latin America.

This occurred partly because bad weather, marked by the shifting southward of the monsoons, affected a thousand-mile-wide strip around the globe, including South Asia and the African Sahel.

Neglect of agriculture and of rural families—who comprise three-fourths of the population in most poor countries—played a part, as those countries tried to industrialize.

Hunger became more widespread also because of larger increases in the population each year. 25 million *additional* tons of grain are needed annually just to keep up with population increases.

Another factor, an "affluence explosion," began to rival the population explosion as a pressure on the food supply. The world reached its first trillion dollars in annual income by 1950. By 1975 the world had roughly *tripled* its real income. Most of the increase went to the wealthy northern regions, including the United States, Canada, Europe, the Soviet Union and Japan. People who could afford it began to eat more meat. To the extent that it comes from animals fed on grain, meat corners a disproportionate amount of food. Rich nations feed more grain to their livestock than the people of India and China combined consume directly, and those two countries represent more than one-third of the human race. The "affluence explosion" has increased the demand for food and for raw materials that make food production possible, has driven prices up, and has made food less accessible to many poor people throughout the world.

2. *Another new feature of famine in the 1970s is the growing awareness that hunger can be prevented.* The spread of new farming technologies, the response to famine by the United States and other countries after both world wars, and the rapid growth of transportation and communications all have made a profound impact. Some of the needed technology is available; food can be distributed; and people hear about this. Hungry people hear about it, too. Where once a fatalistic attitude toward hunger and famine prevailed, people now learn that hunger is not inevitable. That helps to explain why representatives of the poor countries insist on making their voices heard in world forums such as the United Nations when trade, food, population, and other hunger-related issues are discussed.

3. *People have become more aware of world hunger also because food shortages elsewhere hit consumers in the United States with soaring prices—illustrating to each of us the interrelatedness of the world food supply.* This was but one piece of rapidly accumulating evidence in the 1970s that supported the idea of *interdependence.* The environmental movement spread this vision. In other ways so did the oil embargo, inflation, resource scarcities, recession, *detente,* and a range of global devel-

opments that directly affected our lives.

The link between increasing hunger and growing interdependence clearly stirred the minds and consciences of many U.S. citizens. It began occurring to us that our failure to approach problems from a global point of view may be the other side of our inability to cope with domestic problems. Chronic unemployment, crime, expanding welfare rolls, racial tension, spreading slums, neglect of our rural areas, a loss of confidence in the political process, and the bizarre presence of millions of hungry people in the United States are some of the impasses we face. These problems are not beyond solutions, however imperfect, and our inability to deal sensibly with them indicates, among other things, a faulty perspective. It is as though we are lost in a forest at sundown, surrounded by trees that make grotesque, frightening shadows. What we need to do is to see our place in the woods. *A commitment to the whole world, one which begins at the point of people's need for food, would enable us to gain that perspective.* Solutions will then begin to emerge on some of our own internal problems.

The idea is hardly a new one to Christians, who claim a global citizenship. God so loved the *world*, we affirm, that he sent his only Son to redeem it, a Son who had compassion on the hungry and told his followers to feed them. The famines of the 1970s have prompted many believers to take their own faith more seriously in this regard.

The Formation of a Crisis

If the hunger crisis that unfolded in the 1970s illustrates the world's growing interdependence, it also shows that interdependent *action* cannot be taken for granted. If anything, the United States has moved away from such action in recent years, as far as world hunger is concerned. The U.S. response to the hunger crisis, set in the context of events that preceded it, indicate this.

After World War II the United States gave massive food relief to stricken nations and helped in the reconstruction of Western Europe. Europe's spectacular recovery paved the way for optimism—often misplaced—about opportunities for poor countries. Success in Europe, along with unprecedented economic growth throughout the industrialized world during the 1950s and 1960s, conditioned people to think of "freedom from hunger" as a natural development.

In the early 1950s huge grain surpluses began to accumulate in the United States. To solve this problem, Congress in 1954 enacted Public Law 480, which provided for shipments of surplus food abroad, some for sale on easy terms, and some as outright grants. These shipments reached a peak of almost 17 million tons in 1964, much of it helping to avert massive starvation in India. This ready reserve aided—and also lulled.

Several developments followed. During the last half of the 1960s the Green Revolution, which introduced high-yielding strains of wheat and rice, rapidly increased food production in India and other countries.

While this was happening, the United States gradually reduced its costly grain surpluses.

Then bad weather persisted, first in sub-Saharan Africa, where devastation was slow to catch public attention, and later across the Indian subcontinent.

In 1971 per capita food production dropped by 1 percent in the poor countries. Few noticed. In 1972 an alarming per capita drop occurred: 3 percent in the poor countries as a whole, and 6 percent in the Far East, excluding China. The Soviet Union also had a bad year, but no one knew how bad until in 1972 the Russians secretly bought—at an enormous bargain—19 million tons of grain in this country, plus 11 million tons elsewhere. U.S. surpluses were suddenly wiped out.

Prices soared. The price of wheat tripled. U.S. consumers felt the pinch, but extremely poor people around the world faced a calamity. Many, pushed into the "acutely hungry" category, began spending their entire incomes for food. Some died.

October 1973 brought the oil embargo and the eventual quadrupling of oil prices. This had several consequences. It aggravated a *fertilizer* shortage that had already developed. Even at tripled prices fertilizer was not always available in poor countries. In addition, many farmers in these countries could not get *fuel* for their irrigation pumps. Early in 1974, when many of us complained about waiting a few hours for gas, Norman E. Borlaug, winner of the Nobel Peace Prize for his work on the Green Revolution, saw farmers in India who had waited in line two days with tin containers—but the fuel never came. The price of *pesticides* also rose. Many farmers reverted to less productive, cheaper methods of farming, and food production fell.

In this country also, poor people were the worst victims of rising food costs. Studies showed that less than half of those qualifying for food assistance in the United States received any. By June 1974, testimony before the Senate Select Committee on Nutrition indicated that despite substantial new outlays for food assistance during the Nixon Administration, the U.S. poor were becoming hungrier.

The U.S. response to famine abroad was considered critical because most of the world's grain exports come from this country. In 1974 more than half of the grain that entered world export markets flowed from the United States. In this respect our control of grain exports is similar to the control over oil exports that countries of the Middle East exercise.

And we cashed in before they did. The food price hikes followed massive Soviet purchases of U.S. grain in 1972. The oil embargo, with a subsequent jump in oil prices, came in October 1973. The United States was vulnerable to the charge of taking advantage of the food crisis. In 1972 this country earned $7 billion in commercial farm exports. By 1974 that figure had passed the $20 billion mark. More significant, earnings from *poor* countries for farm exports jumped from $1.6 billion in 1972 to $6.6 billion in 1974. The $5 billion increase in earnings, almost all accounted for by the price hikes, was double the total amount of U.S. non-military assistance to the poor countries that year.

Our position appeared all the more Scrooge-like because of several other factors. For one thing, as U.S. earnings from food sales to poor countries skyrocketed, our food assistance to them dropped sharply, primarily because the dollars we budgeted for food assistance didn't buy as much food. The U.S. cutback forced church and other voluntary agencies doing relief work abroad to cut back, too, because most of the food they distribute is purchased by our government. So while hunger and famine—

and our farm export earnings—increased, U.S. food assistance dwindled. It looked like a "sell to the rich and starve the poor" policy.

A second factor put us in a bad light: As food assistance dropped, a larger share of it went to countries in which we had special political and military interests, not countries that needed it most. Secretary of Agriculture Earl Butz said candidly at the November 1974 World Food Conference, where the crisis first fully surfaced, that food is "a tool in the kit of American diplomacy." During the conference he signed a 200 thousand ton food aid agreement with Egypt, where we had a strategic interest. Although Egypt is now among the "most seriously affected" nations, it was not so listed then. In 1974 the United States sent almost five times as much Food-for-Peace aid (Public Law 480 food) to Cambodia, a country with 7 million people, as it did to Bangladesh, a country with 75 million people—even though the need in Bangladesh was far more desperate. The "humanitarian" versus "political" debate prompted one member of the National Security Council staff to argue in all seriousness that "to give food aid to countries just because people are starving is a pretty weak reason." This argument seemed far afield from traditional U.S. generosity.

When the dimensions of the expected famine became clear in November 1974 at the World Food Conference, immediate efforts were begun to fill an emergency "grain gap" that experts agreed would mean the difference between life or death for millions of persons in Africa and South Asia. Speed was critical, because grain shipments were needed during the first half of 1975, and it takes several months to get grain through the "pipeline" to target areas, once a decision to furnish the food has been made.

Immediately after the conference a number of religious leaders and many other citizens urged President Ford to commit at least 4 million additional tons of grain. In February 1975 the President announced an increase of 1.5 million tons (mostly for sale on low-interest terms) to the famine-designated areas. By then India—which had the most extensive shortages—had been forced to use up much of its currency reserves for commercial food purchases. These purchases staved off impending starvation, but invited future hunger because they jeopardized long-range projects such as the development of fertilizer production.

If the unfolding of this crisis shows how interconnected the world's problems are, the U.S. government's initial reactions to it were not encouraging. Our leadership in Washington may never take the far more difficult steps that will be needed to deal with hunger, unless concerned citizens persuade them to do so.

Getting at the Causes

Relief is not enough.

It is one thing to respond to a famine with emergency assistance. It is quite another to get at the causes of hunger with long-range remedies. Both responses are necessary. As the food crisis developed in 1974, many citizens who contribute privately to world relief began asking: "Is this enough?"

They asked it for two reasons. First, they wanted to know what else they could do. Second, they sensed that the problem is so massive that only monumental efforts, aimed at the causes of hunger, will suffice.

Reinforcement for the second idea came in November 1974 when, for the first time, representatives of 130 national governments assembled to deal with the problem of world hunger. They gathered in Rome under UN auspices for the World Food Conference. The participation of virtually all national governments dramatized the fact that whatever else hunger is—and it has many complex parts—hunger is also a deeply political issue. It is political not as a form of partisan politics, but in the sense that unless the resources that governments command are brought to bear on world hunger, it can only get worse.

The World Food Conference proposed a *world food reserve program*, coordinated internationally, but with supplies held nationally. The conference set 10 million tons of grain (plus other food commodities) as the lowest acceptable annual food aid target.

It also asked for a *Global Information and Early Warning System on Food and Agriculture*, which could identify food shortages in advance and provide public information so that governments can take preventive measures. Access to information is crucial. To cite a famous example, Soviet secrecy regarding its food deficit in 1972 led to huge purchases that caught everyone off guard and greatly aggravated the food shortage.

More important, and at the heart of its purpose, the World Food Conference addressed the need for a long-term plan for action. It called for an *International Fund for Agricultural Development* designed especially to help boost the food producing ability, as well as the living standards, of impoverished farm families. By concentrating on the rural poor, the International Fund would seek production gains where they are most needed and where the potential for higher yields is the greatest. The Fund hopes to help (with others) to increase aid for rural development from the 1974 level of $1.5 billion to an annual $5 billion. That is a sizable figure, but modest when you consider U.S. profits from selling food to poor countries, similar earnings from oil by major oil exporting nations, or routine increases in millitary spending.

In order to coordinate these and related proposals of the World Food Conference, the United Nations established the *World Food Council*, with headquarters in Rome.

The conference also called for broader social and economic reforms that will have to occur within poor countries if hunger is to be noticeably reduced, including land and tax reforms that would benefit small farm holders and landless peasants. At the same time the conference asked for a new economic relationship between rich and poor countries in order to stem the widening economic gap that separates them. This points toward areas such as trade, investment and the monetary system. Actions at this level are often the most important and difficult of all.

The World Food Conference gives us a central insight for responding to the question, "What can I do besides give?" The conference implicitly told the average U.S. citizen: Influence government policy. That answer should not discourage giving—private relief and development projects are needed more than ever—but move us beyond it. Among the various ways in which we can do something about world hunger (see Chapters 13 and 14) the most urgent one is to contact leaders in government on issues that vitally affect hungry people. No personal response is more important.

A single action by Congress or one decision by the President can undo—or multiply—many times over the effect of all our voluntary contributions combined. To make an offering in church for world relief and quietly leave the big decisions up to political leaders only encourages them to make *wrong* decisions. Our silence is taken as indifference or hostility when policies are hammered out, and hungry people become victims.

In the early 1960s John F. Kennedy laid out two goals for this nation: One was to get a man to the moon before the end of the decade; the other was to help eliminate hunger "within our lifetime." We accomplished the first goal, but we moved farther away from the more important goal. Why? In large part because those of us who shared Kennedy's vision of a world without hunger failed to take those simple, responsible steps as citizens to translate the vision into a national commitment.

If we cared, we didn't let our leaders know about it, and they acted accordingly.

Each of us can help to change that.

2
Food Production

Imagine ten children at a table dividing up food. The three healthiest load their plates with large portions, including most of the meat, fish, milk and eggs. They eat what they want and discard the leftovers. Two other children get just enough to meet their basic requirements. The remaining five are left wanting. Three of them—sickly, nervous, apathetic children—manage to stave off the feeling of hunger by filling up on bread and rice. The other two cannot do even that. One dies from dysentery and the second from pneumonia, which they are too weak to ward off.

Production and Distribution

These children represent the human family. If present world food production were evenly divided among all the world's people, with minimal waste, everyone would have enough. Barely enough, perhaps, but enough. However, the world's food supply is not evenly divided. The rich 30 percent of the world produces about 60 percent of the food, and consumes about 50 percent of it.

You might conclude from this that the problem is one of distribution, and to a large extent it is. The distribution of food among nations and within nations could be greatly improved through various reforms, all of them complex and most of them long-range—such as providing jobs and incomes that would enable the very poor to buy the food they need. To adequately nourish everyone with present levels of production would take a near-utopian arrangement, and even that would not insure enough food for tomorrow. *Hunger is almost certain to stalk the poor countries until they increase substantially their own food production.*

U.S. citizens generally recognize the importance of food production in reducing world hunger. In fact technology has such an attraction that we are inclined to depend on breakthroughs in food production, combined with a slowdown of population growth, to "do it all." Too often writers encourage this viewpoint by dramatizing new technologies in a way that suggests a solution is just around the corner. Or, failing that, they may paint a doomsday picture. Both approaches make exciting copy. But as a result the U.S. public tends to respond to the hunger crisis like a ping-pong ball, bouncing from one oversimplified conclusion to another. When the famines of the early 1970s occurred, the problem seemed beyond hope to much of the nation. One considerable danger is that a few years of bumper crops may beguile us into believing that hunger isn't so widespread after all. Many will move along to the next social cause.

The importance of food production should be underscored. But a single-minded trust in technology fails to take into account its limitations; and such a trust allows us conveniently to by-pass tough social and political decisions that have to be made. The Green Revolution is a case in point.

The Green Revolution

In 1943, with the help of Rockefeller Foundation funds, a research center was opened in Mexico to develop strains of corn, wheat and beans that could increase that country's food supply. Not only has Mexico multiplied its production of these crops since then, but in the mid-1960s a number of Asian countries introduced a Mexican "dwarf wheat" whose thickness of stem and responsiveness to water and fertilizer made possible the doubling and tripling of yields. These gains, along with the development of high-yield strains of rice in the Philippines, gave birth to the Green Revolution. By 1971, 50 million acres—half of these in India—had been planted in new strains of wheat and rice. Several countries, including India and the Philippines, reached the point of self-sufficiency in these grains. This was a striking accomplishment, though self-sufficiency in these cases meant being able to do without imports; it did not mean raising nutritional levels. In the United States the Green Revolution was widely hailed as the answer to world hunger.

But the poor monsoon of 1972, followed by global shortages of fuel and nitrogen fertilizer, sharply curtailed food production in Asia and elsewhere. Many began to call the Green Revolution a failure.

In fact, the Green Revolution was never intended as a panacea, nor was it the failure that some thought. It did achieve historic gains. It greatly expanded food production and *bought time* for solving other aspects of the hunger problem. It is an on-going revolution, with improved strains constantly being developed. Further, the methods it uses are being applied to achieve similar advances with other crops.

The Green Revolution does not, however, offer the technologies needed for tropical agriculture, or even for temperate zone farming over the long pull. Annual cropping ruins tropical soils, which harden in the sun. High-yield farming in the temperate zones depends heavily on fossil fuel and is especially responsive to fertilizer, not sunlight. We need solar sensitive plant and livestock breeding, both for the tropics now and eventually for temperate zone farming, which cannot rely forever on fossil fuel.

But the Green Revolution's most glaring limitation is not technological at all. Experience has borne out an earlier judgment of Addeke H. Boerma, Director-General of the UN Food and Agriculture Organization, who said that the Green Revolution "does not yet have enough of the general economic and social thrust behind it which we have all along said would be necessary and without which it will fail in its broader objectives for bettering standards of life in the developing countries."[1] The main advantages of the Green Revolution have gone to farmers who can afford to invest in seed, fertilizer, irrigation, pesticides and sometimes machines. Unless poverty-stricken farmers are trained in the needed skills and offered credit on fair terms, they may be driven off the land or back to subsistence farming.

So while the Green Revolution does deal effectively with an important aspect of food production *technology*, it does not pretend to answer the underlying *social* problems of reaching primarily hungry, impoverished rural people. Doing that takes quite a different set of decisions than those made by scientists. Much of the needed technology is within reach. But will it be funded? And how will it be used? And who will reap the harvest? The answers to these questions depend to a great extent on government policy decisions.

Land

Most increases in food production will come from higher yields on presently tilled land, rather than by opening new land to cultivation. An FAO estimate that excludes communist countries says that in Asia, where half of the world's population resides, "practically the entire *potential* arable area will be under the plow" or settled by 1985. Africa and Latin America have huge reserves of land that could be tilled. But in Africa much of it is tropical and requires jungle clearance, malaria and tsetse-fly control, population resettlement, and a great deal of research to develop food production for the tropics. All of these involve time and money. South America has great tropical forests with their attendant problems for agriculture. It also has ready acreage left idle or underutilized, but sweeping changes in land ownership and taxation are needed before suitable agricultural development will occur.

In short, though the estimates vary, a great deal of land remains to be cultivated. The process will be slow and costly, however; and Asia, which needs land the most, can expect to benefit least from new cultivation. Deforestation in India, Bangladesh and Pakistan increases farm acreage—and flooding—which may result in a net loss. Worldwide, much acreage is lost each year to advancing deserts, soil erosion, over-grazing, and to other encroachments, including suburban developments and highways in our own country. In achieving maximum land cultivation, as much depends upon conservation and restoration efforts as upon tilling virgin soil.

The world turned from new acreage to *higher yields* as the major way of expanding food production in mid-century. By the early 1970s higher yields accounted for roughly four-fifths of the increases worldwide. Japan began moving toward intensive (higher yield) farming in the late 19th century, and the dwarf wheat of the Green Revolution owes its initial success to a gene first isolated in Japan. The United States did not make the transition to intensive farming until after World War II. In his book, *By Bread Alone*, Lester R. Brown reports that corn yields in this country actually declined during the first third of the present century. The use that began in the late 1930s of hybrid corn seed and commercial nitrogen fertilizer has since tripled U.S. corn yields. This U.S. crop alone now accounts for one-eighth of the world's cereals and dramatizes the change to high-yield farming.

Soybeans, a high-protein food used mainly in the United States to feed livestock, should provide large gains per acre in the future. High-yielding varieties of soybeans have yet to be developed, but could multiply the output. Another prospect for higher-yield farming is triticale, a tough, productive cross between wheat and rye.

Most gains from intensive farming can and should occur in the poor countries. And it should be *labor*-intensive rather than capital- and energy-intensive, even though capital and energy inputs will have to increase. Asia has only a half an acre of arable land per person, and that ratio is bound to decrease. The experience of China, Japan, Taiwan and others has shown that labor-intensive farming, using the proper inputs and the planting of two or three crops each year on the same land (a method possible in many warmer regions), can multiply the yield. In terms of food production the intensive farming approach, together with gains in tropical agriculture and the development of crops especially responsive to light, offers poor countries their main hope for feeding their growing populations.

Water

The world looks not only to the sky for rain, but also to the oceans and fresh water systems for help in raising food production. Many experts believe that the scarcity of the fresh water supply may do more to restrain food production than the limited supply of land.

Irrigation will expand greatly, but for much of the land presently under cultivation the big irrigation systems have already been developed and in some cases overdeveloped. Not many more deserts are likely to bloom in the next decade or two, because usable water is limited—witness the fight of our southwestern states over rights to existing supplies. Someday the oceans may yield desalinated water for transport to the deserts, but the difficulties and costs now prohibit projects on a massive scale.

The Green Revolution has stimulated emphasis on small tubewells and pumps that farmers can install quickly, rather than on large-scale projects. But even this small-scale technology requires some capital and diesel fuel.

The trend toward small-scale irrigation will gradually be accompanied by a trend toward water-efficient farming as water becomes more scarce. At present, most irrigated land worldwide is devoted to rice, a water-intensive crop. In the future many farmers will turn to crops that use water more efficiently.

Irrigation sometimes brings harmful side effects. Egypt's Aswan Dam has spread a debilitating affliction called schistosomiasis, a parasitic disease carried by snails that afflicts about 200 million people worldwide, including, some estimate, half of Egypt's population. The dam has also caused loss of fertility on land previously flooded each year by the Nile. These problems tarnish but do not disqualify the Aswan Dam as a dramatic example of harnessing water to diminish hunger.

Harmful side effects can often be countered. Lester R. Brown describes one instance in Pakistan in which irrigation had waterlogged a wide area of land and spread salt deposits in the soil. These problems were solved by a system of tubewells that lowered the water table by tapping underground water which, when discharged on the surface, washed the salt downward.

Fish

Since 1970, after two decades of rapid annual increases, the world fish catch has sharply declined. This has been partly, if not entirely, due to the overfishing of many stocks. The cost of fish and competition in the fish industry have increased. The 1973 world fish catch of 65.7 million tons averaged about 34 pounds (live-weight) per person, though the distribution is uneven. The United States alone imports about twice as much fish, primarily in the form of feed for livestock, as do all the poor countries combined.

In the long run the fish catch may increase substantially through such means as the expansion of fish farming or with massive catches of krill, a small shrimp-like crustacean. But the case of krill illustrates the underlying problem for poor countries. As one report noted:

> When krill fishing is finally developed commercially, it is certain to be in the nets of those nations least in need of krill protein—the overdeveloped countries that can afford the enormous expense of mounting Antarctic fisheries—not those that need protein most.[2]

Although fish supply only about 2 percent of the protein in the human diet worldwide, they are still an important source of protein. Better distributed and better used, fish could do much to alleviate hunger.

Fuel and Fertilizer

The connection between food and energy became all too apparent in 1974 when oil and fertilizer shortages aggravated the hunger crisis. The fact that fuel is increasingly needed for food production in poor countries raises serious questions about its use in our own country and its availability worldwide.

The trade-off between energy and food could be agonizing. One acre's corn production requires the energy equivalent of about 80 gallons of gasoline. We could one day be faced with the choice, some believe, of consuming energy on highways and in air-conditioned rooms, or permitting the production of food to feed large populations in Asia and Africa. The trade-off exists between the use of energy for essential food production and its use for nonessential purposes. That important distinction receives emphasis from the fact that on-farm use of energy in the United States accounts for only 3 percent of total U.S. energy consumption.

However, when we move to the entire food system—including the processing, packaging, transportation, retailing, refrigeration and cooking of food—the question of energy trade-offs becomes important. For every unit of energy expended in on-farm production, three units are expended in the processing and distribution of food.

The food system as a whole has become increasingly energy-intensive in the United States. In 1910 that system consumed less energy, measured in calories, than it produced in the form of food calories. But by 1970 the food system required almost nine times as much energy as it produced in food (see the *upper left* side of Graph #1). Corn, soybeans, potatoes, range-fed beef and grass-fed dairy cows still yield more energy than they require in on-farm production (some examples of which appear on the *right* side of Graph #1), but not necessarily when the entire system is taken into account. Most of our corn is fed to livestock, and by the time it reaches our tables in the form of meat, those food calories have consumed their energy equivalent many times over.

Potatoes provide another example. Besides being nutritious, potatoes have good storage qualities and require little processing. But a random visit to a New York supermarket in the spring of 1975 showed fresh potatoes selling for 9 cents a pound, while the cheapest french fries cost five times, and potato chips 20 times as much per pound, although the fries and the chips have lost much of the nutritional value they had as fresh potatoes. The extra cost supports high-energy processing and, of course, the advertising that coaxes us into buying chips in the first place.

Truck farming around cities used to bring in fresh produce, but suburban developments took over much of that farmland, and we have paid for it in more energy and less taste—green-picked, refrigerated and artificially ripened tomatoes, for example. Still, the biggest single inefficiency in the farm-to-table odyssey is that of a two-ton car transporting a bag or two of groceries home.

In a sufficiently energy-abundant world the question of trade-offs between food and energy would not arise. In a world in which energy used inefficiently here could be used in food-deficit areas for food production, the question becomes important.

GRAPH #1

CALORIES INPUT TO PRODUCE
ONE CALORIE OUTPUT

Left of the line is the calorie-in to calorie-out ratio of the entire U.S. food system. Right of the line is that ratio for food production only. Reprinted from the UN *Development Forum*, November 1974. Source: John S. and Carol E. Steinhart, "Energy Use in the U.S. Food System," *Science*, April 19, 1974.

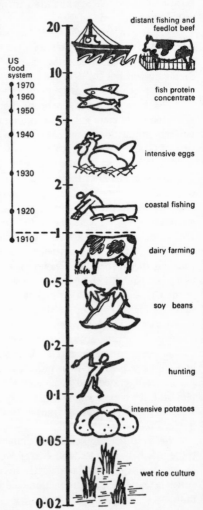

Less use of energy *here* does not necessarily mean more use *there*, however. The transfer of energy to the poor countries requires devices such as assistance, trade reforms or monetary reforms that would enable those countries to purchase the energy, or to develop their own sources of energy.

Commercial fertilizer, the use of which has increased five-fold in the United States since 1950, provides a special link with energy, because nitrogen fertilizer is a petroleum byproduct. The importance of fertilizer for poor countries can be seen by the fact that one ton of it, used on depleted soil there, may result in an additional 10 tons of grain, while an extra ton on already fertilized land in our own country will induce a much smaller increase in yield. But the principle cited above still applies: Less fertilizer here does not mean more there unless transfers are arranged.

The fertilizer shortage began prior to the oil crisis, although the crisis made it worse. The fertilizer industry had overproduced in the 1960s, creating a buyers' market. Some companies went broke. The industry began to *under*produce and prices rose. Fewer companies (including oil corporations) mean more control over production and prices. But should companies have such control over so vital a commodity, when lack of it in countries such as India (see Graph #2) means widespread suffering and death?

What about the Future?

The biggest and most dramatic gains in food production probably lie ahead. The evidence so far, however, tells us to expect most of these to occur along fairly conventional lines, as in the Green Revolution. A similar revolution occurring in tropical agriculture would be an enormous contribution, and it may not be many years away. The use of tropical grasses for beef and dairy cows would be greatly enhanced if tropical diseases could be brought under control. Krill in the Antarctic, buffalo on the ranges, triticale on the plains, cereals that can produce nitrogen in the soil, and high-yield soybeans for human consumption grown throughout the world are some other likely possibilities for food production gains. The development of high-protein cereals and root crops would be especially desirable, because diets

GRAPH #2

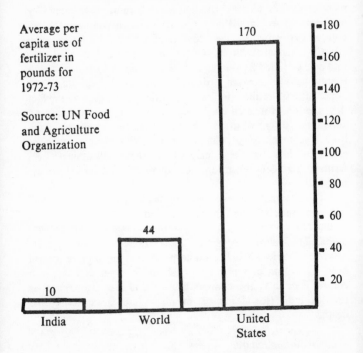

Average per capita use of fertilizer in pounds for 1972-73

Source: UN Food and Agriculture Organization

India   World   United States

for many people in the world have become more protein-deficient—partly because of a trend toward less acreage in beans and peas in several Asian countries.

These gains will take time, however. With 460 million already permanently hungry and more than 70 million additional mouths to feed each year, time is a major factor.

Nonconventional high-protein foods are certain to become increasingly important, but research and production still present formidable obstacles. Single-cell protein, new forms of food from the sea, the turning of starch into protein, the extraction of edible proteins from ordinary grass and leaves—these and other pioneering efforts deserve more support than they are getting.

But the fate of the world's hungry is likely to depend for a long time on less exotic methods of production. The FAO projects the need to increase food production in the poor countries by 3.7 percent each year *simply to keep pace with demand*, a difficult order. This is unlikely to happen unless the United States and other nations get behind the proposals of the World Food Conference and if, among other things, we multiply our assistance for rural development abroad.

More than Technology

René Dumont and Bernard Rosier dedicated *The Hungry Future*:

> To the children of backward countries who never
> attain their full promise,
> or who have died of kwashiorkor,
> because the fish meal which might have saved them
> has fed the chickens gorged by the rich.

As the last two lines imply, it will take much more than food production to deal with world hunger. Peru's anchovy fishmeal industry, the largest in the world, manufactures high-protein flour not for hungry Peruvians, but for shipment to Europe and the United States where it feeds livestock. The fact that Peru needs export earnings so badly that it feels compelled to supply protein to well-fed foreigners, while bypassing its own ill-nourished people, tells us that technology is not the whole answer to the hunger problem. Social and economic remedies are no less essential.

A poor tenant farmer in India cultivates several acres in one or more patches. He works with primitive tools and scavenges manure, not for fertilizer but for fuel. Without irrigation he depends entirely on the rains for a harvest. When the harvest comes, half goes to the landlord, some is stored for food, some for seed, some pays off debts, and whatever remains (if any) is sold to a middleman—who may also be landlord and loan shark —at a deflated price. In a case like this both poor technology

and social obstacles hinder food production. They perpetuate inequalities and reinforce hunger.

Or consider the fact that in poor countries as a whole,
women account for at least half of the food production. Yet
women bear an undue share of the world's hunger and poverty.
Their literacy rate is far lower than that of men, their opportunities fewer. They, too, illustrate that hunger is a social as well as a
technological problem.

Private companies can make an important contribution to
food production, but they do not know how to sell food to people
who are too poor to buy it. Nutritionist Alan Berg has concluded
that "corporate technologists have not yet been able to come up
with a high-protein food that can be sold commercially for a
profit and still be priced low enough to reach and help the
masses of people who most need it."

Hunger does not stand alone. According to Addeke H.
Boerma, head of the FAO:

> It would be futile and unrealistic to attempt to discuss
> hunger and malnutrition in isolation from other evils of our
> age such as the stifling clamp of poverty, the flood of over-
> population, the paralysis of unemployment, the deformities
> of trade. We must look at the economic and social problems
> of the world in their totality if we are to come to grips with
> them individually.[3]

Overcoming hunger, then, means more than increasing food
production, crucial as that is. We also need to sort out hunger's
social and economic allies and deal with them in a comprehensive way. To that task this book now turns.

3
Population

"Why don't people in poor countries quit having so many children? The only solution to the hunger problem is birth control!" writes a mother from the Bronx to Bread for the World, a Christian citizens' movement.

Her letter echoes the thoughts of many. It sounds persuasive. But the argument contains one fatal flaw: It ignores the crucial role that hunger plays in spurring population growth. No country, including our own, has ever restrained a population boom without progress in freeing people from the grip of hunger and poverty. Unless that happens, family planning programs make little impact.

Why?

In most poor countries surviving sons take care of their parents in old age. Faced with a high death rate, and starvation never far away, parents know that many children, especially sons, mean security later on. According to India's former Minister of State for Family Planning, hunger induces women in his country to produce from eight to ten children on the assumption that only three will live to become breadwinners. So the vicious cycle of hunger = more people = more hunger continues to worsen.

The idea that the circle can be broken with family planning measures is a fantasy of the rich world. Paul Ehrlich, whose book, *The Population Bomb*, did much to nourish that fantasy, has since ridiculed it as a " 'condoms from helicopters delusion' —a psychological condition that is rampant among well-meaning upper-middle and upper class Americans."[1] He now maintains that as long as poor couples need sons for future security, family planners' propaganda to "stop at two" makes no sense to them.

First, Ehrlich says, social changes must occur that make fewer children seem desirable.

A bit of historical background sheds light on this insight.

Roots in the West

Almost two centuries ago, in 1798, an Englishman named Thomas Malthus warned that the population would race ahead of the food supply. It would do so, he argued, because we can only *add* to the food supply, while the population *multiplies*. At

GRAPH #3

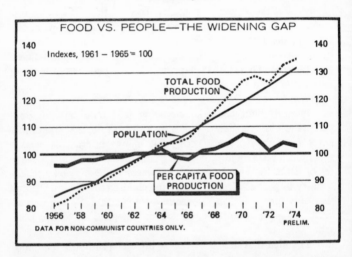

FOOD VS. PEOPLE—THE WIDENING GAP

Indexes, 1961 – 1965 = 100

TOTAL FOOD PRODUCTION

POPULATION

PER CAPITA FOOD PRODUCTION

DATA FOR NON-COMMUNIST COUNTRIES ONLY.

This graph shows that population increases have almost canceled out food production gains. However, it does *not* show increased affluence, which, added to population increases, have made *demand* run ahead of supply by about .7 percent a year for more than a decade. This means that while some have improved their diets, many of the poor eat less. From *War on Hunger*, December 1974. Source: U.S. Agency for International Development.

that time the world's population of less than one billion was growing at a rate of about one-half of 1 percent annually. Now the growth rate is about 2 percent for the world and 2.5 percent for poor countries as a whole. These percentages may seem small, but the increase makes a dramatic difference.

By 1930 the world had two billion people. If you were born in 1930, the world's population has already doubled within your lifetime; and if you live to the turn of the century, you will be able to add still another two or three billion people. *During your lifetime the earth's living population will have more than tripled its previous total achievement.*

That is an explosion.

It explains why the population graphs show a horizontal line veering suddenly upward—as though a cyclist, riding along a barely noticeable slope, began pedaling straight up a cliff.

The world is presently adding 70 million persons each year to its numbers: the equivalent of the entire U.S. population every three years. Most of this growth is taking place in the poor countries, among hungry people. Today's poor countries already contain more than two-thirds of the earth's population. Soon they will contain three-fourths, and by the turn of the century, four-fifths of the human race. All the while demand for the world's food supply will climb sharply each year, and—barring unprecedented global efforts—increasing numbers will wind up in the "hungry" category. No wonder the mother from the Bronx and a great many other U.S. citizens are saying: "The only solution to the hunger problem is birth control."

Consider the evidence, however:

Lower death rates, not higher birth rates, are responsible for today's population growth. Poor countries as a whole have actually lowered their birth rates slightly over the past several decades—but death rates have dropped more sharply, and that achievement has touched off the population boom. Advances in medicine and public health, along with increases in food production, account for most gains against early death. For example, while Malthus wrote his *Essay on Population*, a fellow Englishman named Edward Jenner was discovering a vaccination for smallpox. This discovery foreshadowed a long series of steps in disease control that cut back death rates.

The population explosion began in Europe. Not the "inconsiderate poor" of Asia, Africa and Latin America, but our own ancestors touched it off. A few simple statistics show this. In 1800 about 22 percent of the human race was Caucasian; but by 1930 (only five or six generations later) that percentage had jumped to about 35. This happened because the new technologies that pushed back the death rate occurred in the West. During that time the white, European peoples had two enormous advantages:

1. *Industrial growth kept ahead of population increases.* Because gains in public health occurred gradually, population growth rates also increased gradually. The Industrial Revolution had begun earlier, so the population increase was usually needed in the cities by industries, which depended upon a growing supply of unskilled workers. Although the Industrial Revolution imposed cruel hardships on those who moved from farms to sweatshops and urban slums, the suffering would have been greater and the social situation far more explosive had the population raced ahead of industrial jobs. But the jobs usually got there first.

2. *New lands opened up for colonization.* New lands, including North America, offered an important outlet to population stresses that did develop. For example after the potato famine ravaged Ireland in the 1840s, almost a million Irish came to our shores within five years. When periods of unemployment occurred, new lands provided a place to seek work. They also handed European peoples an impressive psychological advantage by keeping hopes alive.

Poor nations face a sharply different situation today. Two centuries of public health gains were made available to them more rapidly, so their populations began to soar almost without warning. Their people now pour into the cities long before industries can possibly supply them with jobs; and for all but a few there simply is no frontier, no new lands to colonize, no safety valve.

Population growth was cushioned in the West (1) because the death rate receded gradually, and (2) because people became economically more self-sufficient and less dependent upon their offspring for security. Today's poor countries have moved quickly into the first stage: Public health measures and modern medicine have reduced the death rate—but much faster than in the West, causing their populations to multiply more swiftly. *But the second stage is not taking hold.* A majority of people in the poor countries are *not* moving toward the point where their sense of security is clearly related to having fewer children. Instead the opposite usually applies: more children mean more security.

Poor countries can thank us for the population explosion, because rich nations transferred the health technologies that touched it off. But we have not done much to help them develop economies that can absorb new workers and provide positive incentives for small families. We brought them to stage one (a relatively easy task) and largely deserted them in stage two (a far more complicated matter).

To a remarkable extent Malthus has triumphed, because the population is multiplying beyond his wildest fears. Malthus did not foresee how science and technology would cut back the death rate and increase food production.

But in another sense Malthus had things backward. He considered poverty, disease and hunger important though regrettable checks on population growth. So he assailed English welfare legislation (called "poor laws") on the grounds that they only encouraged the poor to have more children. However, history has since contradicted Malthus. Where people are poor, diseased and hungry, the population soars. Disease and infant mortality have been restrained enough in underdeveloped areas to multiply growth rates—but not enough to assure parents that sons will survive to care for them in later years.

Once a country begins to reduce its death rate, it *has* to go on to reduce hunger and poverty as well, or face a runaway population. *Only where the benefits of healthy economic growth are spread among the poor, and where the rate of infant mortality approaches that of the rich nations, do people feel secure enough to have small families.* This happened in our own country, in other industrialized countries, and it is beginning to happen in a few countries that are successfully developing. Adequate nutrition, health care, literacy, and improved incomes for the poor emerge as the most fundamental remedy to the population problem.

This does not minimize the importance of family planning. Nor does it ignore the possibility that disaster or deprivation can, under special conditions (that of Ireland following the famine, for example), provide incentive for smaller families. It does, however, affirm that no country has yet brought a rapidly growing population into balance primarily by promoting private methods of control. Conceivably, of course, pressures of growth combined with dramatically improved birth-control methods could change that. But the evidence so far tells us that to expect poor countries to solve their population problem by emphasizing family planning is to cherish an illusion.

Some Examples

The experience of poor countries over the past several decades is revealing. Those that have substantially lowered high population growth rates are countries in which the poor have noticeably improved their living conditions. Countries, however, in which the poor remain just as poor and the hungry just as hungry are stuck with stubborn growth rates—regardless of whether birth control measures are pushed or not.

Consider China and India, which together have more than one-third of the world's population. Both are very poor. But China, with 800 million people, has distributed its resources so that food, housing, health care and education are made available to all. According to reports (which are far from complete) China has virtually abolished hunger. China's annual population growth rate may be somewhere between 1.7 and 2 percent—still too high, but substantially lower than before; and although small families are encouraged and family planning services available, the underlying control seems to be a dependable, though stringent, system of social and economic security. If the Chinese continue to improve their standard of living, the population growth rate will probably continue to decline.

India, the first poor country to officially promote family planning programs, has faltered. These programs haven't made much difference overall. Many of India's 600 million people suffer acute hunger. Many are illiterate and unemployed. As a result, India's growth rate remains at 2.5 percent annually. But within India several states—including Kerala, one of the poorest —have cut back the growth rate significantly, and these are the ones that show exceptional evidence of reducing hunger, making health care available, and increasing the rate of literacy.

In South Korea and Taiwan, birth rates dropped sharply as living standards began to improve, and this happened in advance of active family planning programs. For example, Taiwan's birth rate fell from 46 per thousand in 1952 to 31 per thousand in 1963. That year Taiwan launched an official birth-control program; but the birth rate has fallen only slightly since then, a decrease that may be due more to economic gains than to the programs.

Many countries have higher per capita incomes, but poorer distribution of incomes and social services than South Korea and Taiwan. Consequently they also have higher population growth rates. In 1971 Brazil's per capita income was $395, South Korea's $280. But in Brazil the income ratio of the richest 20 percent to the poorest 20 percent was 25 to 1, while in South Korea the ratio was only 5 to 1. Brazil also had higher rates of illiteracy, infant mortality and unemployment. Both countries had population growth rates of 3 percent in 1958, but by 1971 Brazil's held at 2.9 percent, while South Korea's had dropped to 2 percent. South Korea had the advantage of a birth-control program, but, like Taiwan, most of its drop coincided with economic gains by the poor and came *prior to* the program.

What should poor countries do about their rapid population growth? Your answer may depend on where you live. In September 1966, the Committee for Economic Development issued two reports that dealt with the problem. The report prepared by a committee of 44 North Americans urged birth control programs. The other, prepared by nine Latin Americans and one U.S. citizen, favored improved nutrition and reduced infant mortality—with the U.S. member registering the lone dissent. Commenting on these reports environmentalist Barry Commoner notes:

. . . the Latin Americans wish to pursue, for themselves, the course toward population balance that the advanced na-

tions have followed—increased living standards, reduced
mortality, followed by the commonly experienced reduction
in birth rate. For their part, the North Americans are urg-
ing on the poorer nations a path toward demographic balance that no society in human history, certainly not their
own, has ever followed. . . .[2]

An even more striking example of the "here" versus "there"
perspectives emerged in 1974 at the UN-sponsored World Population Conference held in Bucharest. The United States strongly
urged poor countries to push family planning programs, warning
that they would become mired in permanent hunger and poverty,
and that the earth's carrying capacity had limits.

Poor countries, on the other hand, argued that social and
economic improvements were the key factors, understandably
preferring to deal with population growth the way the developed
countries have. Representatives of the poor countries pointed
out, sometimes scathingly, that excessive consumption practiced
by the rich nations contradicted their preachments about the care
of the earth. Numerically, population increases are greater in the
poor countries, they observed; but in terms of resource-consump-
tion and pollution, growth in rich nations takes a much greater
toll. "You want us to cut back on population?" some asked.
"Then you cut back on consumption."

The U.S. position at Bucharest contained valid points; but
they would have gotten a more receptive hearing if they had been
placed within the context of urgent development needs in the
hungry world. Not doing so has been, as the mother from the
Bronx illustrates, a national blindspot. At Bucharest the United
States stood almost alone in failing to see the connection between motivation for smaller families and social-economic development.

The evidence leads us neither to minimize the problem of
population growth, nor to downgrade the importance of family
planning. But it does warn us against dealing with population
growth as an isolated problem, apart from the hunger and poverty that induce such growth. If we are serious about dealing
with the population problem, our sensible course, as a nation,
would be to take a whole network of actions designed to let peo-

ple work their way out of hunger and poverty.

Within the framework of such a commitment several points deserve emphasis. First, the elimination of hunger and poverty within our own borders must be part of a global effort to slow population growth. Second, we need to reassess a way of life in which excessive consumption has become a national addiction that engulfs us all and strains the carrying capacity of the earth no less than population increases do. Third, we could invest in more research to develop quickly birth control methods that are dependable, inexpensive, simple, and morally acceptable to all.

But the main point is that efforts to bring the population growth rate down will be effective only as part of an overall assault on world hunger and poverty.

"Lifeboat" and "Triage"

How many people can the world adequately sustain? No one really knows. Much depends on undiscovered reserves, alternate sources of energy, new technologies, our ability to change patterns of living, and other factors that prompt a variety of guesses. This uncertainty provides a field day for alarmists. If you conclude that the earth already has too many people, your solution is apt to be a bit reckless—as two widely discussed arguments show.

One, made popular by scientist Garrett Hardin, pictures the rich countries as lifeboats filled to near capacity. If more people are pulled in, the lifeboats will sink and everyone will drown. So those in the lifeboats have to push away others who are trying to climb in. By this view, to feed the hungry and bring them medical care is to overload the lifeboats and, therefore, precisely the wrong thing to do.

The other argument, suggested by William and Paul Paddock in their book *Famine 1975!*, uses a military idea called "triage." The world is like a battlefield covered with wounded soldiers, but not enough medics. What to do? (1) Some will die no matter what help they get. Abandon them. (2) Others can survive without treatment. Ignore them, also. (3) Help only those wounded seriously who can be saved by immediate care. Applied to the hunger-population dilemma, triage means deciding which countries are beyond assistance, starting with India and Bangladesh, and letting their people starve.

But do these metaphors apply? Why lifeboats instead of luxury liners to illustrate the rich nations, for example? Triage, the more sophisticated of the two, has rightly been called by *The New York Times* "one of the most pessimistic and morally threadbare intellectual positions to be advanced since the demise of the Third Reich." According to the same *Times* editorial, "the world has yet to make a really serious effort to crack the food crisis."[3] It points out that starvation prompts a compensating rise in birth rates, while assistance to small farmers and landless laborers results both in more food and in a lower birth rate.

Behind the lifeboat and triage theories lie some frightening, unspoken assumptions about the value of life. Is a hungry, impoverished Asian child less human, with less reason to live and less right to live, than our own children? Playing God in this regard is especially dangerous because we are easily seduced by answers that protect our own advantages, even if they cost lives. Those who believe each person to be an incredibly precious human being, created in the image of God and redeemed by him at great cost, will see in population growth not merely problems, but persons: children of God.

The population growth rate *is* a critical problem, but we can deal with it in a way that affirms and celebrates life. So far, the most effective way to bring the growth rate down has been to bring down hunger and poverty. And that requires major legislation by Congress to carry out, among other things, the strategy of the World Food Conference.

Part II
Bread and Justice

4
"Haves" and "Have Nots"

We will not deal effectively with hunger through private acts of charity alone. It is possible for us to feed a hungry family or two—an action not to be despised—without disturbing the conditions that brought about their hunger. In order to make lasting gains against hunger, the concern from which charity flows must also give rise to justice.

Put another way, we should care enough about hungry people to ask *why* they are hungry. And if we ask that question, the answer is as simple as it is complex: People are hungry because they are poor. We cannot come to terms with hunger unless we deal with poverty. And we cannot understand poverty apart from a rapidly growing gap between the haves and the have nots of the world.

Their Poverty and Ours

Poverty in most countries defies the imagination. Peter Drucker has said:

> What impresses the outside world about the United States today is not how our rich men live—the world has seen riches before, and on a larger and more ostentatious scale. What impresses the outside world is how the poor of this country live. "Up to Poverty" is the proper slogan. . . .[1]

Drucker has a point. Where in our own cities do you see—as you can in India—people carrying buckets of water from or bathing at public water taps, emaciated cattle wandering in the streets, women scooping up piles of dung for use as fuel, children picking out undigested grains from the dung for food, people sleeping in the streets, urinating in the streets, begging in the streets, competing for garbage in the streets, and dying in the streets? British journalist Dennis Bloodworth tells of the time he first brought his oriental wife Ping to London. "Don't show me more museums," she told him, "Show me poor people. I want to see how poor people in West live." So Bloodworth showed her the slums of London, only to find her exasperated. "No," she protested, "You don't understand, I mean poor people, *reary* poor people."[2]

In ordinary times really poor people go hungry. When the price of food goes up, their ranks swell and deaths increase. The list below shows the average percentage of disposable income that people from various countries paid for food in the early 1970s:[3]

United States	17%	Indonesia	50%
Great Britain	22%	Peru	52%
Japan	23%	Zaire (Congo)	62%
Soviet Union	38%	India	67%

More is at stake than percentages. 17 percent of $10,000 is one thing; but 60 percent of $300 is quite another.

Why Poor Countries Cannot Repeat Our Experience

Not only is the poverty of most nations far worse than poverty within the United States, but today those countries cannot hope to climb to prosperity by duplicating our experience, because the experience of the Western world has been misleading. There is no use telling them: "Do it the way we did it." Scientist Georg A. Borgstrom points out:

No group of individuals ever seized a greater booty than did the Europeans who took possession of the vast forests and rich prairie soils of the North American continent. Unassuaged, the white man also grabbed the fertile pampas and most other good soils in Central and South America, the South African veld and the rich highland plateaus of the interior Africa. He managed to gain control of an entire continent, Australia, with its valuable satellite, New Zealand. In addition, he secured strongholds all over Asia where he monopolized trade and to a considerable degree controlled agricultural production. . . .[4]

Grade school history lessons about conquerors, colonizers and empire builders taught us how European people gained control of most of the world by the turn of this century. We learned this and took it in stride, forgetting that the same history had quite a different meaning for those who were conquered. For example, Bengal (today's Bangladesh and the West Bengal state of India), the first territory that the British conquered in Asia, was a prosperous province with highly developed centers of manufacturing and trade, and an economy as advanced as any prior to the industrial revolution. The British reduced Bengal to poverty through plunder, heavy land taxes and trade regulations that barred competitive Indian goods from England, but gave British goods free entry into India. India's late Prime Minister Nehru commented bitterly, "Bengal can take pride in the fact that she helped greatly in giving birth to the Industrial Revolution in England." British rule became comparatively enlightened and brought some advances to India such as Western science. But, as India illustrates, the North Atlantic powers seized territories and privileges to enrich themselves, not to benefit the local population.

New lands not only boosted Western economies, but they also provided a safety valve for Europe's growing population. We can imagine the burden for Europe if all its living descendants—virtually the entire population of the United States, Canada, much of Latin America, plus Australia and some European colonies in Asia and Africa—were compressed into Europe. North America in particular was a huge breadbasket waiting to be farmed, a storehouse of natural resources made to order for the Industrial Revolution.

Lester B. Pearson, former Prime Minister of Canada, reminds us what a difference these advantages made when the

North Atlantic nations were struggling to develop:

> One hundred fifty years ago, most economists doubted the capacity of the new Atlantic-European industrial system of that epoch to survive. What transformed mid-century gloom into the long Victorian boom was, above all, the opening up for settlement by Atlantic peoples of the world's remaining, virtually unoccupied belt of fertile temperate land. This biggest bonanza ever bestowed upon a single group was purchased for little more than the cost of running the Indians and the Aborigines and the Bantu off their ancestral lands. It temporarily ended the Malthusian nightmare of population growth outstripping resource availability. Its vast input of almost "free" resources took the Atlantic countries past the borders of modernization and into the new territory of "sustained growth." Nothing comparable is available to developing nations today—unless we use our abundant capital and technology to provide a comparable form of aid relevant to our times. If we say they must develop without it, then we are really abandoning them to permanent helplessness and poverty.[5]

Pearson adds, "Their nineteenth century bonanza gave the Atlantic peoples, representing less than 20 percent of the world's population, a grip on the planet's resources which they have since maintained and even strengthened."

Today's poor nations have no comparable outlet for their populations, which are increasing far more rapidly than Europe's ever did. They do not have the input of wealth, science and energy that characterized growth in Europe and North America, an input obtained in part at the expense of the poor nations. They face the difficult task of pulling themselves up from poverty at a point in history when forces are sucking them deeper into it.

In these countries most migration occurs not to lands of opportunity, but to cities of last resort. Until recently cities in Europe and North America grew along with industries that supplied jobs. But poor countries now experience the opposite: peasants pour into cities far in advance of employment opportunities. Too few industries exist, and some hire only skilled workers because they are already automated. "Hands" are no longer as marketable as they were earlier in our own history.

U.S. citizens clearly build on unparalleled advantages. The merchants, farmers, factory workers, and housewives of our country enjoy a level of prosperity that is possible only because the past has granted us unprecedented favors. We have been living off the labor and resources of others more than we realize. Inherited economic and social advantages, not moral superiority, explain why the average personal income in the United States reached $5,606 in February 1975, a figure that amounts to $22,424 a year for a family of four. Because earnings are unevenly distributed, a majority of U.S. families earn far less than that. The fact remains that hungry people of the world do not have the advantages that paved the way for these achievements.

A Widening Gap

In comparing rich and poor nations today we are pressed to use the crude measuring device of either per capita national production (GNP) or per capita income. But this country's GNP includes research and development of highly polluting technologies, as well as the cost of repairing the environmental damage caused by those technologies. Both are counted as part of the nation's output, although one should be subtracted from the other. Similarly, traffic jams raise the GNP by boosting gasoline sales, auto repairs, and medical expenses. GNP figures may also distort in the sense that a haircut in the United States may cost ten times the price of a haircut in India—but a haircut is a haircut. Despite these distortions, per capita figures provide us with a fairly clear idea of where wealth and poverty are concentrated.

The (Pearson) Commission on International Development reported that 34 percent of the world's population has more than 87 percent of its GNP. That leaves two-thirds of the human race with 13 percent of the world's output. Further, under this breakdown "rich" nations include countries that by our standards are poor. An industrial worker in Russia, for example, worked 10 times as long as his U.S. counterpart in 1971 to purchase a refrigerator, 17 times as long to purchase an orange, 9 times as long for a dozen eggs, and 4 times as long for a pound of beef. Compared to the extreme poverty of poor countries, however, the Soviet Union is properly classified as wealthy.

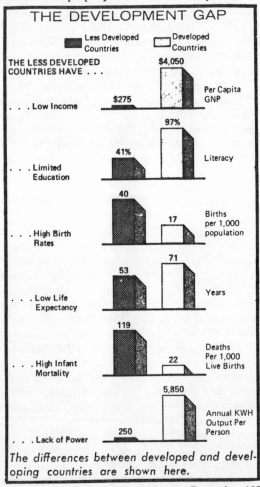

1974 estimates, from *War on Hunger*, December 1974.
Source: U.S. Agency for International Development.

In 1974 Exxon revenues of $42 billion exceed the GNP of all but three poor countries: China, India and Brazil. GM's 1973 sales of $36 billion almost tripled the total output of Pakistan and Bangladesh combined. 1973 revenues of $23.5 billion for AT&T more than doubled the GNP of the Philippines. Many U.S.-based corporations are higher producers than most poor countries.

Moving away from GNP's, New York City, with a population under 8 million, has an annual budget almost the same size as that of India, a nation with 600 million people.

Even more distressing than the *size* of the gap between rich and poor nations is that the gap continues to increase, not only in total amounts, but in *percentages* as well. Two centuries ago the average per capita income of the richest countries was perhaps eight times greater than that of the poorest. But today's average U.S. citizen has an income level a hundred times that of his counterparts in Bangladesh. India's per capita income went from about $64 in 1953 to $100 in 1973, while in the United States the figures from those years jumped from $2,100 to $5,015. In poor countries as a whole, from 1960 to 1970 the average per capita income increased by 27 percent, compared to 43 percent in developed countries.

The distinction between increases in *total* amounts of growth and *percentages* is critical. There is no chance of narrowing the gap in terms of total amounts for many years without almost stopping, or reversing, growth in the rich countries, a situation that would probably set poor countries back even futher. Per capita income in the United States is about 50 times that of India; so a 1 percent per capita growth here means an annual increase of roughly $50 per person on the average, while a growth rate ten times higher in India would only increase incomes by about $10 per person. Clearly to suggest an immediate narrowing of the gap in real terms would seem to nourish a misleading hope. We could, however, change the *kind* of growth that takes place in all countries, and tip the *percentages* of growth in favor of the poor countries.

As alarming as the income disparities *between* rich and poor nations is the fact that gap-widening usually takes place *within* poor countries as well, where the affluent few absorb most of the gain. Rapid population growth accelerates this trend by depressing wages through an oversupply of workers and by inflating land values and rents, as space becomes harder to secure. A widening income gap within underdeveloped countries shrinks already limited annual gains to pennies for the poor, and in many cases makes them poorer than before. Partly because of this "severely skewed income distribution" the World Bank concluded in its 1972 annual report, made before the hunger crisis sharply worsened: "As a generality, it is probably true that the world's burden of poverty is increasing rather than declining."

Since 1972 the sudden rise in food and oil prices has put the poorest nations in a worse position than ever. These make up what is now often called the "Fourth World"—countries that, unlike other Third World countries, have neither oil nor other compensating advantages that enable them to cope with the new economic dislocations. These nations especially reflect a growing maldistribution of income. Their suffering sharpens Lester B. Pearson's warning that our planet cannot survive "half-slave, half-free, half-engulfed in misery, half-careening along toward the supposed joys of almost unlimited consumption."[6]

5
Environment, Resources and Growth

As the need to move swiftly and effectively against hunger increases, two new complications have surfaced: (1) the struggle for a clean environment; and (2) resource limitations. They affect both rich and poor nations, but pose special dilemmas for the poor ones, who find themselves facing additional handicaps when the deck has already been stacked heavily against them. Both dilemmas demonstrate that the struggle against hunger moves us inescapably to a quest for social justice.

Save the Environment: Two Movements

The campaign to save our environment mounts pressure against poor countries to pay an extra price as they industrialize: the cost of pollution control. For that matter, the pressure is felt on low income people in our own country and at times has surfaced in public clashes between those fighting for jobs and those fighting to conserve nature.

In reality *two* environmental campaigns are going on. One centers primarily on protecting nature and its ecosystems. The second concerns itself with social ecosystems that produce hunger, disease, and crowded hovels. By logic these two indispensable campaigns deserve to unite and strengthen each other. In practice they often collide.

The first campaign is being waged by those who are not so poor, some of whom are more indignant about smog than about slums, more worried about the mistreatment of animals and lakes than about mistreated people. This tends to pit the rights of nature against human rights. A higher passion for nature is not surprising, because most U.S. citizens suffer from its abuse. Fewer of us are shorn of basics like food, shelter, medical care, work, income, and mobility.

In contrast, the second environmental struggle is prompted (if not always led) by those whose lives are battered by lack of these things. They have always struggled against nearly impossible odds, and now a new hurdle is being placed in their way. Another fee is being exacted. Rich people are upping the ante on them again. The poor of the world would probably like to breathe better air and keep their waterways pure, if they had decent jobs and enough to eat. But pollution-free hunger does not appeal to them.

In the United States the attempt to reverse environmental damage may no longer be postponed. But it does exact a high price, and the question is: Who will pay the bill? Barring clear measures toward assured employment and a more even distribution of incomes, the burden will fall excessively on those with low and moderate incomes. The wealthy will be only marginally affected and poor people will go on expecting the fight for our natural surroundings to divert attention from *their* environment.

The conflict between nature-environmentalists and poverty-environmentalists is even more intense at the international level, with far greater stakes for the poor countries. The stakes are high, first of all, for them to keep nature in shape. A report by former UN Secretary-General U Thant, which prompted the United Nations to convene a world Conference on the Human Environment in Stockholm in 1972, itemized the horrors of failure, such as an estimated 1.25 billion acres of productive land lost through erosion or salt poisoning.

The stakes are also high in the cost of repairing or preventing damages. Consequently many poor nations feel saddled with the dilemma of having to choose between an immediate need to reduce poverty and a long-range need to preserve the environment—with pressure on them from us to prefer the latter. But if poor countries have to shoulder the whole burden of protecting their environment, when they are already struggling against hunger, they may understandably conclude that "protecting the environment" is another name for staying hungry.

In 1971 Norman E. Borlaug, a key figure in the green revolution, criticized "irresponsible environmentalists" who insist that DDT and related pesticides be banned from further use. The danger of DDT is widely known. It does not readily decompose, so its components are not recycled harmlessly into the earth. Instead it finds its way into the food chain and ultimately into human bodies in increasing (though as yet very minute) quantities. Borlaug asserted that this danger has been exaggerated and that a ban on DDT would mean increased hunger and starvation in the underdeveloped countries. The Food and Agriculture Organization also considers DDT and similar pesticides vital for food production in many countries and says that "until cheap, safe and efficient substitute pesticides are produced and made easily available, there is no alternative to the judicious use of DDT, especially in the developing world, to increase agricultural productivity to feed the growing number of people on our planet."

Are the environmentalists right in sounding an alarm on DDT? They probably are. While the extent of danger is subject to widely different interpretations, it would be foolish for us to take chances. DDT cannot be recalled like cars with faulty brakes. It enters the soil and water to stay—or to make its way into the food chain.

Are Borlaug and FAO right in arguing that such pesticides are vital to food production in the underdeveloped countries? Until effective alternatives appear, they are. What we have, then, is an impasse between urgent concerns that clash head on: one an immediate necessity, the other a long-range danger. If the past is any indication, immediate necessity will not be pushed aside. People who lack food will gladly take risks on DDT.

The above example is not an isolated one. The United Auto Workers sponsored a symposium in preparation for the 1972 UN conference at Stockholm. The symposium turned into a debate between youthful environmental enthusiasts and representatives of underdeveloped countries. "They say in Seoul, Korea, the smog is a mark of progress. It shows you're making it in American terms," complained a young Yale graduate. He had more to complain about. According to an ambassador from Ceylon, "Two-thirds of mankind, who live in the developing regions of the world, do not share the same concern about their environment . . . as the other one-third who live in the more affluent regions." He said that pure air, fresh waters, and beauty would not be acceptable substitutes for economic progress. The delegate from Trinidad agreed. "I keep telling my colleagues that industrial pollution is not our problem, we would like to have more of it. . . ."[1]

Industrial pollution is the touchiest question, because poor nations are being asked to pay costs that the rich nations did not bother paying while they became rich. At Stockholm, after bitter debate on whether or not underdeveloped countries should receive some compensation for additional costs of environmental controls, the industrialized nations, led by the United States, voted no. The cost of controlling pollution amounts to a sizable new industrial tax. With underdeveloped countries severely pressed to industrialize faster, they can hardly be blamed for resisting a cost that makes industrial expansion more difficult. Of course, those countries must take care of their environment or incur debts for its neglect. At the same time they are under strong pressure to postpone payment—like we did—and concentrate now on economic development. That type of borrowing involves serious and uncertain risks for the world, but a "pay now, eat later" policy does not strike them as entirely fair.

The way to resolve this dilemma is to work it out on the basis of a unified world view. The logic of the natural environment, as well as the logic of human justice, calls us to deal not with separated parts but with the whole world. In that case the nature-environment and the poverty-environment movements will each have to adopt the cause of the other as part of its own.

But the main burden falls on the nature-environment people to humanize their outlook and campaign for human justice, because they can do so without the distraction of putting hungry children to bed. Otherwise, affluent people will certainly turn environmentalism into a self-serving and probably self-defeating enterprise. If the interdependence of life includes first and foremost the interdependence of people, then true environmentalism embraces freedom from hunger. That is the kind of movement on which both rich and poor nations need to unite.

Resource Limitations and Economic Growth

Although warning signs were on the horizon earlier, it was not until 1974, when the oil embargo, oil price hikes and global food shortages made their full impact, that the U.S. public came to realize that we could no longer take an almost unlimited supply of cheap natural resources for granted. Food prices went up here, while famine abroad provoked steady news coverage. The world's grain reserves dipped to their lowest point since the years immediately following World War II.

Oil prices, while grating to many of us, served notice that, except for new finds, known oil reserves could run dry within a matter of decades. One could hardly blame the otherwise impoverished Arab countries for getting what they can from a resource that might be theirs for a couple of generations at the present rate of consumption. The oil squeeze pushed this country to pursue alternate, costly and (especially in the case of nuclear power) controversial sources of energy.

Because manufactured nitrogen fertilizer, the chief commercial type, is a petroleum by-product, oil prices aggravated an already developing fertilizer shortage. Pesticides, as a derivative of crude oil, also became more expensive. Add land and water as resources whose availability for additional food production is diminishing, and you have, in the case of food, a striking example of a resource scarcity that is related to the scarcity (or low availability) of other resources as well.

Food and energy are at stake, but so are other basic raw materials. Just as the food shortage led to the UN-sponsored World Food Conference in November 1974, so earlier that year the oil crisis prompted the United Nations to convene a special session of the General Assembly—not, however, merely on oil or energy, as the U.S. government hoped, but on raw materials in general. At this special session poor countries called for "a new international economic order" in which they would have adequate control over and fair prices for their raw materials, and assurance of long-range development opportunities.

Lester R. Brown has pointed out that the United States is already dependent upon imports for more than half of its supply of 6 of the 13 basic raw materials required by a modern economy. By the turn of the century the United States is expected to import most of its supply of all but one of these.

U.S. Dependence on Imports of Principal Industrial Raw Materials, With Projections to the Year 2000

Raw Material	1950	1970	1985	2000
	(per cent imported)			
Bauxite	64	85	96	98
Chromium	n.a.	100	100	100
Copper	31	0	34	56
Iron	8	30	55	67
Lead	39	31	62	67
Manganese	88	95	100	100
Nickel	94	90	88	89
Phosphorus	8	0	0	2
Potassium	14	42	47	61
Sulfur	2	0	28	52
Tin	77	n.a.	100	100
Tungsten	n.a.	50	87	97
Zinc	38	59	72	84

From *The Global Politics of Resource Scarcity* by Lester R. Brown. Washington: Overseas Development Council, 1974. Source: U.S. Department of the Interior publications.

The question of supply limitations involves a wide range of resources and a great many uncertainties. For example, to what extent will additional reserves of oil be discovered, or alternate sources of energy developed? It is too early to say.

One thing is certain. The question of resource availability, following on the heels of the environmental movement, has pushed to the forefront a debate about economic growth. The outcome of this debate—measured not in oratory but in hard-nosed decisions—will have far-reaching consequences for billions of present and future people who fall into the "hungry" column.

The limits-to-growth debate began in 1972 when interlocking problems—more people, limited resources, multiplying demand for them, increasing pollution—prompted an appeal strange to Western ears: restrain growth. In a document called *Blueprint for Survival*, 33 British citizens detailed a proposal for "a stable society"—that is, a society without economic or numerical growth. Two months later a group of scientists, sponsored by the Club of Rome, published *The Limits to Growth*. Using global data, they projected by a computerized "systems analysis" the distant consequences of continued growth. The starting assumptions fed into the computer were pessimistic on such things as the discovery and development of new resources, and the possibility of greatly reducing pollution—assumptions which rigged the outcome and brought heavy criticism ("Garbage in, garbage out," complained one critic.) Each model led ultimately to sudden collapse of growth either because of food or raw material shortages, or because of pollution. These scientists concluded that the only way to avoid an abrupt collapse would be to plan ahead for absolute limits on population, pollution, and production. That, they contended, means gradually halting economic growth.

Although the thesis that a nongrowing society offers the only alternative to ecological disaster has attracted a vocal following in this country, it has been adopted by relatively few scientists and is almost universally rejected in the poor countries. Global ecology is an infant science and its data still fragmentary. We know that the world's natural resources are not infinite. We hope to effectively harness solar energy and to make better use of additional raw materials, although estimating the extent to which we succeed at such efforts necessarily pushes us into guesswork.

Either a no-growth or a slow-growth future would create a sizable problem for the United States—but nothing like the crisis it would present to poor countries. If there is to be a slow rate of growth, for example, how is that growth to occur? Would the rich nations limit their own consumption of raw materials so that the poor nations could process a larger share? Or would we lock the poor nations into starvation? That prospect is by no means remote, since most estimates concede that the earth's present population will soon double. If the rich nations *now* gobble up a lopsided share of new economic growth, then under conditions of *reduced* economic growth could poor nations look forward to getting even smaller portions for their swelling populations? Clearly, to propose a leveling off of growth raises the question of where that growth is to be concentrated. And that, in turn, pushes distribution of wealth to the forefront as an urgent issue.

The answer seems to lie in *more discriminately planned growth* in order to secure harmony with nature *and* justice for people. Such an approach postpones the question of the limits to growth, but it is the only effective way we have of working out an answer to that question. Meanwhile the assessment of the late Paul G. Hoffman, who once headed the UN Development Program, probably applies, that "increased productivity is necessary for providing both the financial and the technical resources to undo the environmental damage that has already been done."[2]

The heart of the matter concerns not the quantity but the quality of growth. Concentrating on the quality of growth may or may not slow the rate of growth. According to environmentalist Barry Commoner, "What happens to the environment depends on *how* the growth is achieved." By itself, halting economic growth could still be part of a formula for environmental disaster. As Commoner points out in *The Closing Circle*, the dramatic increase in U.S. environmental pollution since 1946 has occurred not primarily because of population growth or increased production, but because of new, pollution-intensive technologies which place unprecedented burdens on the life systems of nature. It is above all these technologies (for example, those involved in the production of synthetics such as plastics, fabrics, and pesticides) that have to be dealt with if we are going to make peace with our environment.

What kind of growth do we want? Should Detroit build more gas-guzzlers or convert to durable economy cars and vehicles for mass transit? Should we base our decisions on a surfeit of clever advertising that whets our appetites for products we do not need, in ever increasing amounts? Or can we concentrate on essentials and turn more of our labor force to service jobs that would improve our education, health services, parks and the like? We might be able to change a situation in which the United States, with 5 percent of the world's population, consumes about a third of the world's energy and minerals. We could have a growing economy that emphasizes improving the quality of life.

Style of Life

Concern for our stewardship of nature, along with discomfort over the fact that our 5 percent of the human race consumes more marketable wealth than does the poor 70 percent of the world, has prompted many to re-examine their style of living. The thrust, however modest, is toward a more sparing, less materialistic way of life.

The Christian tradition has valued (though Christians have not always practiced) simplicity of life and voluntary poverty, ideals drawn not least from Jesus himself, who had "nowhere to lay his head." It is expressed daily in the lives of millions of ordinary Christians, some with church-supported vocations, but most from the ranks of the laity. They have chosen to share what they have with others in response to the Gospel. The chief value of doing so is spiritual and symbolic—which is not to say "rather than real," as though spiritual and symbolic actions accomplish little. The transfer of resources involved is relatively limited. The power behind such commitment consists in lives that are placed more fully at the disposal of God and other people, and in keeping alive for others a sense of proportion.

Life-style adjustments should not, however, be viewed as a substitute for helping to enact needed public policies. Putting less fertilizer on your lawn and contributing the savings to a good cause may be useful for a variety of reasons, but in themselves these actions are congenial to the present hierarchy of wealth. They do not tinker with questions of justice. Regarding the environmental movement Barry Commoner writes: "What is just beginning to become apparent is that the debt [to nature] cannot be paid in recycled beer cans or in the penance of walking to work; it will need to be paid in the ancient coins of social justice—within nations and among them."[3]

Consider the example of energy. U.S. air-conditioners alone consume as much energy as does the entire nation of China with its 800 million people. On a per capita basis we use twice the energy that West Germany does and three times that of Japan. Peter G. Peterson, former Secretary of Commerce, reports that according to the Federal Energy Office this country wastes as much energy as Japan uses. Turning down our thermostats and driving less may have an integrity of their own, but even if widely practiced they are not apt to cut back extensively on energy waste. To be effective, energy conservation must result from carefully designed national policy, have the force of law, and be applied to the nation as a whole. We need, then, to move from the personal to the public realm on such a matter.

The waste of food in the United States provides an almost endless list of horrors that, in turn, suggest ways in which we could conserve personally on this precious commodity. Each U.S. citizen consumes on the average about 1,850 pounds of grain per year, compared to 400 pounds in poor countries, mainly because we consume most of ours indirectly as meat and dairy products. According to the U.S. Department of Agriculture, in December 1974 the average pound of edible beef in this country represented seven pounds of grain. As a result the idea of "eating lower on the food chain" by cutting back on grain-fed meat makes sense, but doing so does not automatically transfer food to hungry people. The grain "saved" may be sold to feed Russian livestock or simply not planted next year by farmers who are worried about low prices. Food will reach hungry people only if government policies see to its proper production and distribution, so an adjustment in eating habits without responsible citizenship may prescribe failure and hurt family farmers.

Adopting a more modest style of life can be a powerful witness in the struggle against hunger, if efforts to change public policy accompany it. Unfortunately too many people attracted to a life-style approach want to stop there. Life-style changes appeal as immediate, personal responses. But they can also lull us with a false sense of fulfillment. Not having a television set because most people in the world do not have one, or not using sheets on our beds because few of the world's poor can afford them, can be morally satisfying. Unless such actions are accompanied by more positive steps, however, they may do nothing more than put people out of work.

The appeal that is primarily needed is not for less personal consumption, but for a greater share of per capita U.S. growth. Therefore the most important sacrifice that readers of this book can make is the sacrifice of their time and energy to change public policy. A life-style adjustment may be useful, but detached from attempts to influence government policy it tends to be an ineffective gesture. Our sense of stewardship must become sufficiently large to include both.

6
Up from Hunger

"Sir, I'm hungry!" pleaded a five-year old boy in Addis Ababa, Ethiopia.

He had approached Bernard Confer and Leslie Weber, both Lutheran executives engaged in world relief. They turned, and as Weber tells it, "I had no doubt about his being hungry. He wore a single cloth garment and his eyes bulged. I reached in my pocket and gave him a coin. Soon there were other children and my Ethiopian money was gone. My friend Confer commented, 'You have helped these children today, but who will help them tomorrow?'"

Who will help them tomorrow?

Or to ask the question underlying that one: How can we deal with the *causes* of hunger? What are its long-range remedies?

Because hunger springs from poverty, gains against hunger require development, the kind of development that enables people to climb above the most wretched forms of poverty.

The Development Struggle

Despite obstacles, seemingly unsurmountable at times, poor countries are not yet locked into despair. They still hope to work their way out of hunger, but doing so requires a combination of heroic effort on their part and greater cooperation on the part of other countries, including and especially our own.

Fortunately we are not starting from scratch. During the past three decades, while most of today's poor countries achieved their independence, a great range of development efforts took place. Results have been mixed, because the efforts were not

58

always sufficiently wise or comprehensive; nevertheless, tens of millions have risen above the level of malnutrition and absolute poverty. They are the real measure of these efforts. In the process, nations and international agencies have worked together and accumulated a rich backlog of experience. Because the United States played a central role in opening a large flow of development assistance, we can find satisfaction in knowing that many more people would be hungry today without these initiatives.

In the process we have learned some of the things that work and some that do not. For example, we now know that a high rate of economic growth does not insure the kind of development that reaches the masses of poor people—although no one has figured out how development can occur among poor people without economic growth, either. During the decade of the 1960s—called the first UN Development Decade—poor countries as a group averaged an increase in economic growth of 5 percent a year, a growth rate higher than that achieved by today's rich countries, when they were in the earlier stages of development. Yet the gap between the "haves" and the "have nots" widened and more people were poor at the close of the decade than when it started.

Can we learn from this that development should occur primarily among the poor, and be measured less by the Gross National Product than by the quality of life? The world cannot contain five or ten billion persons consuming resources as rapidly as people in the United States do. But even if that were possible, would it be desirable? Christians who understand God's concern for the whole person and for the whole world should be especially conditioned to reach for a more human view of development, both here and abroad, than one that fastens mainly on income or production.

A country in which health services are available to all may be more highly developed than one with a more favorable ratio of physicians and hospitals, if these serve only the well-to-do. A country with beaches and parks for the public could be considered more advanced than one in which superior natural facilities are cornered by a minority of property owners. A country able to feed, house and employ its people adequately may be much better off than a wealthier country with a booming economy and a wasteland of hunger. In short, development should be measured primarily by what happens to people on the bottom half, not the top half, of the economy.

Efforts to develop along these lines meet with obstinate resistance, both from within poor countries and from elsewhere. One internal obstacle to development is *neglect of agriculture*, which will be examined more carefully later in this chapter. Another internal obstacle is *attachment to the status quo*. Persons with wealth or power to preserve, corrupt officials or merchants, or poor people who fail to understand the causes of poverty and passively accept their lot in life may all resist needed changes. A third is *poor allocation of resources*—in capital-intensive industry, for example, when capital is scarce and labor abundant; in show-case development projects; or in excessive military spending. Other internal obstacles may stem from the period of colonialism, when systems of education, communications, transportation, commerce and even food production were created for the purpose of exporting cheap raw materials or cash crops to the controlling country, not for local development. To reflect even a bit on these obstructions is to realize how difficult it is to overcome them.

Not all obstacles to development lie within the poor nations, however. Many are still imposed on them by the rich countries. These external obstacles, which also reflect the reluctance of those with advantages to give them up, include: (1) trade and investment practices that stack the deck against poor countries; (2) scarcity of genuine development assistance; and (3) "cultural colonialism" by which rich nations impose on poor countries growth-distorting values or systems—schools that prepare a few for college, but leave the rest ill-equipped to be better farmers or workers; or advertising that develops a craving for luxury products, from Cokes to cars, rather than for basic commodities.

These obstacles to development threaten to bury the poor world in a permanent sea of misery. They have to be dealt with candidly by both rich and poor nations through the adoption of positive alternatives. For this reason I will sketch an approach to development that begins where most hungry people still live: on the countryside.

Accent on Agriculture

Much of the world goes hungry because farmers and farm workers are a neglected majority. Even in the United States, 40 percent of our poor live in rural areas, although only one-quarter of the population is rural. But in underdeveloped countries *three-fourths* of the population lives off the land. To reverse a saying of Jesus: the laborers are plentiful but the harvest is few.

One good result that could emerge from the famines of the 1970s is the turning of attention to agriculture, where a revolution of attitudes, changes in practice, and many more resources are needed. Bringing this about will not be easy, although the World Food Conference made an important step in that direction.

Farmers living on a subsistence level or barely above it understandably resist change, when one miscalculation can destroy the thin security which their traditional habits insure. Paul E. Johnson, Operations Division Chief of the Office of Food for Peace, relates this experience:

When I was in Afghanistan 15 years ago, we tried to get the farmers to advance from the sickle to the scythe. A team of three Austrians worked at it for four years; a very capable young Swiss farm-tools technician with FAO spent two years on the project. After all this the Afghan farmer continued to use the sickle. Using the scythe he could cut as much wheat in an hour as he could cut with the sickle in 3 or 4, but the scythe shattered more of the grain and reduced his net yield slightly. With only an acre or two of land and with wife and children to help him in the field, labor costs were not important, but each teacup full of wheat was important in feeding hungry mouths until the next harvest.[1]

No matter how much he may want to better himself, a farmer eking out a marginal existence cannot afford to gamble. Improvements have to be demonstrated, and must be part of an integrated program of change that offers him a social and economic security more dependable than the one he is asked to give up. The eagerness with which farmers grabbed hold of "green revolution" technologies shows, however, that given clear opportunity for improving their conditions, farmers adopt new methods as readily as anyone else. That some abandoned those technologies in 1974, when shortages and costs drove them out of reach, underlines the need of farmers for security.

Improvements can give a farmer pride in himself and in his vocation. As of now, most countries suffer at every level from a bias against agriculture, and ambitions are directed away from rather than toward it. Speaking about this, agriculturalist Norman Borlaug says, "The miseries of life on the land are such that once you get an education you want to become a doctor or a lawyer or professor—anything but an agricultural scientist."[2] This attitude toward agriculture has become institutionalized by leaders in government, business, and the professions, who feel exactly the same way about farm work as the peasants do. "The agricultural adviser should be the main instigator of technical progress," writes René Dumont in *The Hungry Future*. "But in Africa he is a comparatively underestimated official and all he wants is a position in the capital, after a period in Europe. He is not nearly so well treated as his colleagues in the Health and Education Departments."[3] Dumont reports an experience with an Asian agricultural adviser who refused to go into the rice fields, in order to keep his shoes from getting muddy.

Poor countries need a national goal for rural improvement and an idealism that prompts workers with a broad range of skills to go to farms and villages to involve rural people in development.

Swiftly climbing unemployment explains in part why rural development must get urgent attention. Driven by hunger and poverty on the countryside, and lured by visions of a better life, millions flow to the cities each year looking for jobs. Too often the jobs aren't there. Families settle in shantytowns, and if unemployment persists, broken homes, alcoholism and crime may follow. In the poor countries urbanization is taking place at a far more rapid rate than it ever did in Europe or the United States. Once again today's poor are "getting there too late"—at a time when industry tends to move toward high-cost, labor-saving technology. To find something like it in the United States you turn to the migration from the rural South of several million impoverished blacks, who arrived in the cities when unskilled hands were no longer in demand. Because our situation has never been honestly faced, it has generated difficulties far out of proportion to the original problem. Still, it is microscopic compared to the migration now going on in the underdeveloped countries.

The rising demand for food and employment, plus the fact that most hungry people live on the countryside suggest these steps:

1. *A labor-intensive approach to agriculture.* Poor countries *do* have people who need work. They do *not* have capital to buy machinery that is not essential. Fortunately most improvements toward higher production, such as higher-yield seeds, fertilizer, irrigation, second-cropping, terracing, improved plowing and weeding, and harvesting higher yields, require mainly additional labor. More labor is also necessary for roads, storage and supply centers, schools, clinics, and a host of other improvements. The evidence is abundantly clear that small-scale, labor-intensive farming can usually bring higher yields per acre than large-scale, mechanized farming.

2. *Land reform.* In many poor countries, farm families own little or no land and have neither the means nor the incentive to increase production. The situation varies from area to area. In India, farms have either gotten larger through mechanization or been carved into smaller and smaller units under the crush of population growth. Either process creates more landless workers who are often serfs in lifelong debt to their landlord. In Latin America, owners of huge estates seldom invest their profits in rural development, and what little the governments get from them in taxes seldom goes there, either. Millions are left without hope or incentive.

If land reform is essential for development in so many countries, why is it so widely ignored? Because prosperous landowners don't like it. Imagine the resistance in our own country to a movement for chopping up corporate farms or Southern plantations into smaller family units. Conservative leaders in Latin America chafed when President Kennedy had land reform written into the principles of the Alliance for Progress in 1961. They ignored it, and after Kennedy's death, land reform dropped from the language of U.S. officials as well.

3. *Industrial development that is related to rural develop-*

ment. The tendency has been to forget agriculture and develop industries. It hasn't worked. But putting industry to work for agriculture, and vice versa, spreads gains throughout the entire population. For example, industry can concentrate on manufacturing fertilizer, tools, and other products vital to farming. Industry can also develop along labor-intensive lines. Much of it can be located in rural centers for turning out basic products, such as clothing and furniture, that use mainly local materials and local skills.

The experience of the West during the Industrial Revolution deserves emphasis. It is ironic that people in the underdeveloped countries who want to copy Western industrial patterns tend to downgrade agriculture, overlooking the fact that integration of industry and agriculture was central to development in the West. Initial stages of industrial growth in Europe and North America depended upon earlier agricultural development, and as farmers became consumers, they helped to spawn industries not directly related to agriculture. Today, as well, countries need agricultural development as a base for industrial growth.

What are the consequences of slighting agriculture and neglecting rural life? Doing so hinders food production and distribution. It insures that the income gap will continue to widen in most developing countries. It stimulates migration from farms to cities, transferring unemployment and poverty to places where they are even more difficult to cope with. If the world's hungry are to eat well, and if development is to have meaning for more than a privileged minority, then the overall strategy of emphasizing agriculture makes sense.

Models of Development

Efforts to develop show widespread diversity. No two countries are alike, and the great majority of poor nations avoid lining up in the camp of either communist-type socialism or unrestrained capitalism. Most try to find their own path, with practical considerations playing a much bigger role than economic theories.

In Latin America Brazil stands out as an "economic miracle" with an annual growth rate of 10 percent for seven consecutive years, from 1968 to 1974, and no sign of slowing down. But Brazil's Minister of Finance said candidly in 1972 that only 5 percent of the population had benefited from the country's economic growth, and that same year *The Wall Street Journal* reported that most of Brazil's people were as poor or poorer than when the boom began. According to a 1974 analysis, unchallenged by the Brazilian government, the real purchasing power of the bottom two-thirds of the population had been reduced by more than half over a ten-year period. Brazil reflects a guided, but relatively unrestrained type of capitalism under the direction of military dictators.

Cuba, the Latin American version of communism, has wiped out hunger and unemployment. It has lifted its farm workers out of dismal poverty and offers health care, education and economic security to all citizens. Food and other products are severely rationed, and absenteeism from work and school runs high—a phenomenon unheard of in China. Cuba depends heavily upon the Soviet Union economically, although by 1975 improved prices for sugar and other exports had diminished that dependency. Civil liberties are no more famous in Cuba than in Brazil.

Chile, traditionally one of the most prosperous and democratic countries in Latin America, found itself with a duly-elected Marxist president in 1970. Salvador Allende won a plurality, but not a majority of the votes in a three-way contest. Allende tried to help Chile's poor to substantial improvements; but high inflation, opposition from the middle and upper classes, and other factors (some would include political ineptitude or outside pressures) led to Allende's overthrow. A hard-line military regime seized power in September 1973. By early 1975 Chile had widespread hunger and unemployment, and still an annual inflation rate of several hundred percent.

In Africa Kenya and Tanzania, neighbors on the eastern coast, illustrate approaches to development on that continent.

Kenya, endowed with more abundant natural resources, has chosen modified capitalism, welcomed most foreign investments, and since 1964 has had an average growth rate of about 6 percent a year. But Kenya faces the problems of mounting unemployment and an unfavorable balance of trade.

Tanzania, with an annual per capita income of less than $100, is carving out a distinctively African type of socialism. This country lays heavy emphasis on cooperative villages based on the tribal custom of communally held land. It is one of Africa's few democracies. Both Kenya and Tanzania were hit by the drought of the late 1960s and early 1970s, and at the World Conference Tanzania was named one of the five most critically grain-deficient countries.

In Asia, Japan stands out as the country that "made it," China as the country "making it," and India as one doing neither as yet.

Japan became a rich, developed nation while most of today's poor countries were still colonies. It has special advantages: a nontropical climate and social cohesion that helped Japan fend off attempts by the West to make it a colony. Drastic reforms, including land reform, paved the way for industrial growth, and Japan achieved a kind of national partnership in which government, banking, industry and labor work together: a benevolent capitalistic version of central planning. Diligence and a literacy rate higher than our own are two of Japan's assets, but this country's weakness lies in heavy dependence on imports of oil, food and other raw materials. Still, Japan offers some hope to nations with limited natural resources.

China concentrated on modern industry in the 1950s and millions streamed to the cities to find neither jobs nor housing—a familiar story. Then in a major policy switch China decided to wrap its development efforts around agriculture and allied industries. By the middle 1960s economic recovery had clearly taken place. Now 800 million Chinese, with an annual per capita income of perhaps $165, are moving toward development unassisted.

Our knowledge of China is much too limited, but visits by specialists since 1971 reveal impressive gains. *Life* correspondent John Saar noted a level of overall poverty but saw "no hunger, no untreated sick, no beggars"—an observation verified by others. Gone, too, are the prostitutes and opium smokers. Swollen eyes and open skin sores no longer plague the peasants. City streets and villages are immaculate. Unemployment has been eliminated, and although wages are meager, everyone is assured housing, education, medical care, and food. As reported today—and some caution is needed because of limitations placed on visitors—China gives a picture of people moving with a sense of dignity and purpose in a setting of austerity. The world has never before witnessed an attempt on such a scale to build a new society from the bottom up.

On the negative side, China's experiment shows a passionate totalitarianism that harbors little dissent. With a highly centralized, authoritarian government, China has the ability to industrialize with some speed through "forced savings"—in a manner not altogether unlike that of the capitalists of the Industrial Revolution in the nineteenth and early twentieth centuries, who extracted enormous profits from the sweat of the workers, profits they kept investing in more industrial expansion. Even so, this kind of go-it-alone development presupposes mineral resources needed for industrialization, and a great variety of skilled technologists—conditions few other countries enjoy.

The Chinese model is one of repulsion-attraction to the rest of the underdeveloped world. Its harsh regimentation repels, but then the Chinese have to arrange life with perhaps one-thirtieth of the per capita wealth that we enjoy.

India's plight can be quickly illustrated: more people than Africa and South America combined, an annual per capita income of about $100, urban unemployment that is expected to exceed 50 million by 1980—and a national budget scarcely larger than that of New York City. Nearly half of the population lives below the official poverty line, which in India is almost a starvation line. The caste system (illegal but alive) and other traditions, including a diversity of languages, make development difficult. India's blend of free enterprise and socialism has not always worked well, though economic theory may have little to do with that. Despite these and other deficiencies, India has shown great resilience and capacity for growth.

A "New Economic Order"?

What kind of world do we want to help build, not just in the fantasy of idle dreams, but with personal efforts? If we seek a world in which even the poor are able to work and eat and live on at least a minimally decent level, a world that in the long run has a reasonable chance of holding together with its humanity intact, then a greatly expanded program for development makes sense. At best this will be a long, hard struggle stretching well beyond our lifetimes. And it will mean making sizable accommodations to poor countries without delay.

Poor countries, too, are asking: What kind of world do we want to build? They, through considerable hardship, also see the need for accommodation on our part. To them it is a matter of simple justice. Understandably they are no longer waiting passively for rich nations to take the initiative. They are bringing their case to the court of world opinion, in public forums such as the United Nations, and using economic leverage where they have it. As oil showed, for some countries the leverage lies in their raw materials, which industrialized nations depend upon.

The UN General Assembly's special session on raw materials in April 1975 issued a declaration for "a new international economic order." Backed primarily by the poor countries, the declaration seeks a system that would assure them of (1) control of their own natural resources; (2) fair prices and open markets for their exports; (3) increased development assistance free of political or military conditions; and (4) an adequate flow of resources for their development. Included in the last item is reform of the monetary system so that, for example, a link is established between development and Special Drawing Rights. SDR's are international credit reserves created by simple agreement for the purpose of financing trade, but since they were first issued in 1970, three-fourths of them have gone to rich nations.

These principles are not unreasonable, though achieving them will not be easy. The prosperous countries might well have pursued them years earlier, had they placed the ending of hunger seriously on their agendas. Now both industrialized and developing nations are smarting from oil price increases; but in early 1975 some oil exporting countries were offering to negotiate decreased oil prices in return for new rules in the world economy, along the lines indicated above, that would benefit the poor countries.

Because most countries—rich, poor, and oil-exporting—have a huge stake in a better world economy, the food and energy crises could set the stage for agreements to achieve that. Doing so will take a combination of pushing on the part of poor countries and willingness to make concessions on the part of our own and other affluent countries. The cost to us will not be small. But what kind of future, what judgment of God, do we invite if we fail to move in this direction?

The Gospel and Human Justice

Concern for human justice may seem to many to be far afield from the Gospel of Christ. Not at all. What prompts Christians to respond to others is God's love and visible human need. God's love sets us free to care deeply about others, so when their need confronts us, we act. But if our faith and love are genuine, we will want that action to do more than make us feel good or bestow temporary relief. We will want our action to deal with their need as effectively as possible. Dealing effectively with hunger clearly pushes us into the public policy arena, into questions of social justice.

Grounding our ethic in the Gospel, we affirm for others a right that we enjoy: the right to food. We want the hungry to overcome a situation that flagrantly violates their humanity. To see them not secretly as inferiors, but truly as brothers and sisters of the same heavenly Father, is to earnestly desire their full human dignity as his children. Christian concern, then, precisely because it springs from the Gospel, moves us to seek the justice that God invites us to celebrate.

Part III

The Need for a U.S. Commitment on Hunger

7
The Rediscovery of America

The United States is a great country and a generous country, but we have drifted away from our own tradition of generosity. As a nation we are not seriously trying to help the human race overcome hunger. We have no vision for joining with poor countries to arrange a more livable world.

Retreat from a Hungry World

The vision is not beyond reach. It has occasionally been sketched by our leaders, but for the past decade they have studiously avoided summoning the nation to act on any such vision. Secretary of State Henry A. Kissinger provided two striking examples in 1974. At the UN Special Assembly on Raw Materials, in April, he told the world:

On behalf of President Nixon, I pledge the United States to a major effort in support of development. My country dedicates itself to his enterprise because our children, yours and ours, must not live in a world of brutal inequality.

"We are part of a large community," he said, "in which wealth is an obligation, resources are a trust, and joint action is a necessity." Later, at the World Food Conference in Rome, Kissinger proposed the goal "that within a decade no child will go to bed hungry," and urged joint action "to regain control over our shared destiny. If we do not act boldly, disaster will result from a failure of will."

In each case the words appeared to signal a major initiative by the United States, but no such initiative came. We continued to pursue policies that, for example, left us near the bottom among donor countries, when development assistance is measured as a percentage of national production. And early in 1975 Congress voted another cut in such assistance.

The Role of U.S. Ideals

This retreat from the world of hunger has been accompanied for more than two decades by the enlargement of U.S. military power. *But the strength of the nation lies more in its ideals, and in the practice of those ideals, than in the flexing of national muscles.* Put another way, power is nothing new. The world has seen power as long as nations have existed, sometimes trembling before it, sometimes submitting to it, but never loving it. Others have loved the United States, but seldom for its power. Rather what captured the admiration of people throughout the world was the fact that, for all its faults and contradictions, this country wrested its independence from England and started a new experiment in freedom. In setting out the nation's course, its founding leaders declared that "all men are created equal," and they determined to shape the nation's destiny along democratic lines.

To invoke national ideals is not to deny fundamental departures. Freedom for the colonists and pioneers also meant freedom to seize land from the Indians, and to make slaves or second-class citizens of black people. These violations of human dignity have left ugly and abiding scars. But at least it is possible to recognize them as contradictions to be resolved, because they fail to harmonize with the principles upon which the nation was established.

Those who settled in our land came with no unified set of principles. They were dissenters, religious refugees, acquisitive people, adventurers, people fleeing depression and famine, fugitives from justice, rich and poor people, good and bad. They represented a host of national and cultural backgrounds. But they made this a country where freedom and democracy were celebrated, if not always honored in practice. The United States of America was more than a new nation. It became a *movement* rooted in the equality of man, and embodying the hope of "liberty and justice for all."

The terms liberty, justice and equality have deep biblical roots. When applied by a nation they do not deal with the relationship between God and his human creatures, but they do draw heavily from the implications of that relationship and from the biblical view of the Kingdom, and therefore they are ideals that Christians and Jews have special reason to cherish.

The lessons of the nation's past tell us that liberty and justice cannot be secured for ourselves and kept from others without turning sour. Because we have cherished liberty for others, this country has sacrificed enormously (if not always wisely) in lives and material resources. We have not cherished justice as much. But justice and equality are no less a part of the nation's ideals, and we build on them by exercising them in our relationship with others. When we are rich and others are hungry or impoverished beyond description, justice calls for ending this imbalance.

Strength versus Power

Internally and internationally, the strength of our nation lies in its ideals. Without them we are like Samson shorn of his hair. Unfortunately we have relied increasingly on raw power. Contrary to some critics, the shift toward power was not cynical. In part the circumstances of history thrust it upon us, and in part it grew out of a misunderstanding. Until the end of World War II, much of the poor world knew the United States as the champion of self-determination. To many we were heroes. We stood for an end to colonialism and for freedom to the colonies. After World War II a new factor emerged—the extension of communist domination over Eastern Europe and success of the communists in China. The communist takeover in Eastern Europe and the threat of similar developments in Greece and Turkey were viewed with alarm as a new form of colonialism, and as such prompted a vigorous military buildup under our sponsorship, beginning with the NATO countries of Western Europe.

This militant anticommunist stance took place as the *con-*

tinuation of our opposition to colonialism. But it locked us into an oversimplified interpretation. The communist revolution in China, for example, did not turn out to be part of a Soviet conquest, but a nationalist uprising with hard-line Marxist ideas. In fact the Soviet Union reacted to "losing" China far more intemperately than we did. (We vilified our China experts, Stalin executed his.) The same oversimplified interpretation, however well motivated, prevented us from understanding Vietnam and led to the tragedy of military intervention there.

Vietnam can only be understood against a century-long background of colonialism. Like most of today's underdeveloped world, Indochina was gobbled up by a European power. France, anxious for the grandeur of empire, forced its way into Vietnam in 1857 and fought for decades to control Indochina. Armed resistance never disappeared in that colony. The Vietnamese, unified somewhat by language and by a long history of opposition to Chinese invaders, drew strength from a nationalism already well established.

Under France, the gap between rich and poor widened. In *Asian Drama* Gunnar Myrdal reports:

> The Vietnamese were generally excluded from the modern sectors of their economy as well as from higher posts in the government. Banking, mining, large-scale manufacturing industry, and rubber production were jealously guarded French preserves. . . . In addition, French settlers, usually of peasant stock and with a background of service in the lower ranks of the French army, acquired large amounts of land. . . .[1]

Myrdal also found that "Frenchmen of lower-class origin" occupied positions in government and business for which, by contrast, the British in India trained Indians. This practice of the French excluded the Indochinese still more.

France fought movements toward eventual self-rule, so moderate nationalism had no chance to emerge in Vietnam. France prohibited political parties and trade unions. The consequence, writes Myrdal, "was to leave the underground Communist Party in the forefront of the Vietnamese struggle for independence." The French, who in effect recruited for the communist movement, could claim that in fighting Vietnamese nationalists they were fighting communism.

President Roosevelt wanted France out and Indochina independent, much to De Gaulle's displeasure. In 1944 Roosevelt wrote to Cordell Hull:

> France has had the country—thirty million inhabitants—for nearly one hundred years, and the people are worse off than they were at the beginning. . . . France has milked it for one hundred years. The people of Indochina are entitled to something better than that.[2]

In 1947 Secretary of State George C. Marshall advised France to make peace with Ho Chi Minh on generous terms, and warned that continuing the war or attempting to set up a puppet government might play into the hands of communists throughout Asia by putting democracies in a bad light. Despite this warning, the United States began to support French colonialism once more, paying for 80 percent of France's war by 1954 and then finally—as far as the Vietnamese understood it—replacing France as the colonial power.

One reason we misread Vietnam, ironically, is that our record of colonial rule (in the Philippines, for example) was benevolent compared with that of the French. As a result we failed to understand the intense feeling of the Vietnamese against foreign intervention, or why our intervention, so well intended in the eyes of most of us, should meet with such hostility. So instead of encountering a situation analagous to Korea, in Vietnam we reaped the consequences of a century of French misrule and found ourselves defending corrupt regimes that had little popular support.

Vietnam illustrates, rather than contradicts, the fact that our military commitments abroad and the enormous sacrifices these entailed were motivated primarily by a desire to prevent another colonial power (or powers) from gobbling up helpless countries. In the process, however, the United States has placed itself in the unpopular role of world policeman, accused of practicing the colonialism we sought to prevent. Because that role involves a shift away from influence by example and toward influence by power, it obscures our ideals, and in the long run undermines our purposes.

The use of the struggle against communism as our primary tool for measuring situations abroad is a mistake for several reasons. It is a negative approach; we define ourselves by what we are *against* rather than by what we are *for*. That distorts. We cannot base a convincing program on our ideals and project it to the world by stressing what we oppose.

The approach is also based on fear. It shows an excessive awe of communism and too little confidence in democracy. We must be realistic and recognize the threat which the communist mixture of totalitarianism and idealism still represents. We cannot ignore what happened to Hungary and Czechoslovakia. But the facts fail to support a position of abject fear, of mental paralysis. Do not setbacks to communism during the 1960s in many poor countries, because of domestic reactions against it, dispel the myth of communist invincibility? Do not fundamental splits between communist countries likewise lay to rest the phantom of a unified international movement against us?

In addition this negative approach is wrong because the problems that communism depends upon for winning converts—hunger, poverty, repression—are successfully attacked not with guns, but with social reforms and economic gains.

Our preoccupation with anticommunism has also moved us toward the support of too many totalitarian regimes, a stance that clearly violates the ideals we want to promote. To talk about ideals is not enough. Echoing President Johnson on Vietnam, President Nixon assured the nation that we were "only fighting for the right of people far away to choose the kind of government they want." But the runner-up to President Thieu in South Vietnam's 1967 election was in prison; and Thieu's one-man contest in 1971, followed by various repressive actions, showed that nothing of the sort was happening in Saigon. Further, while Nixon spoke, the United States was shipping arms to the Pakistani government, which was engaged in savage repression of the people of East Pakistan (now Bangladesh), who *had* expressed their will in contested elections. We cannot expect developing nations to be immediate, mature, full-blown democracies; but our policies should encourage a free expression by the people in any country.

Greece, the birthplace of democracy, is another case in point. In 1967 a group of army colonels seized power, suspended constitutional rights and shut down parliament. A thousand-page report by the 15 nations of the Council of Europe, which later expelled Greece from the Council, documented cases of brutality and torture. Washington, however, ignored the Council and in 1970 resumed full shipment of heavy arms to Greece. Business, as well as the government, was implicated when in April of 1971 Secretary of Commerce Maurice H. Stans spoke in Athens before high-ranking government officials:

> We in the United States government, particularly in American business, greatly appreciate Greece's attitude toward American investment, and we appreciate the welcome that is given here to American companies and the sense of security that the government of Greece is imparting to them.[3]

Overthrow of the Greek military leaders in 1974 left the United States widely discredited in Greece, as democratic elements regained control.

Too much reliance on power, coupled with fear of communism, has even led us to take part in misguided military interventions. Vietnam is not the only example. The year 1961 found us deeply involved in the Bay of Pigs fiasco in Cuba. In 1965 the U.S. Marines invaded the Dominican Republic to dismantle a reformist revolution that had seized power. Regarding that, former Senator J. William Fulbright has written:

> The central fact about the intervention of the United States in the Dominican Republic was that we had closed our minds to the causes and to the essential legitimacy of revolution in a country in which democratic procedures had failed. The involvement of an undetermined number of communists in the Dominican Revolution was judged to discredit the entire reformist movement, like poison in a well, and rather than use our considerable resources to compete with the communists for influence with the democratic forces

who actively solicited our support, we intervened militarily on the side of a corrupt and reactionary military oligarchy. We thus lent credence to the idea that the United States is the enemy of social revolution, and therefore the enemy of social justice, in Latin America.[4]

Anti-communism as the guiding star of our foreign policy leads us to positions that are foolish when measured by traditional U.S. ideals. Consider, for example, our "tilt" toward Pakistan in 1971 because of its militant anti-communism. After the Pakistani army had for eight months committed crimes that forced ten million Bengalis to flee into India, President Nixon publicly commended that country's ruler, then General Yahya Khan, for his efforts "to reduce tensions in the subcontinent." Meanwhile an even more astonishing example was shaping up in Chile.

In 1970 Chile elected by plurality a Marxist President—a distasteful outcome for many U.S. citizens. The fact remains that Salvador Allende was elected through the democratic process by the voters of Chile, and he worked within that process. The United States immediately moved to cut Chile off from crucial financial credits, food assistance and spare parts for machinery, such as trucks and farm equipment, bought in the United States. That part of our response was legal, if deplorable. But the Administration also authorized more than $8 million for secret efforts, through the Central Intelligence Agency, to make it difficult for Allende to govern, thus paving the way for his overthrow. After the takeover by a hardline military dictatorship, credits and assistance to Chile were promptly restored.

Detente might apply to the communist superpowers, but not to a tiny democratic country that dared to elect a socialist government. We clearly preferred a dictatorship and interfered to bring it about.

These examples show that the leadership of *both* political parties has erred in its eagerness to bolster governments that set themselves against communism, but in doing so it has not led the United States to pay "a decent respect to the opinions of mankind," which the Declaration of Independence commends to us. Because public opinion also represents great power, this has weakened our influence in the world community.

Most important of all, our preoccupation with communism has led to "benign neglect" of hunger and poverty, a neglect which fails monumentally to keep faith with the nation's ideals. Adrift from these moorings, we have lacked the capacity to participate in a global development program of the magnitude and quality that would once again evoke deep admiration for the United States. Anchored in our ideals, we could easily ensure a massive, worldwide effort to reduce hunger and poverty. Providing such leadership entails changes in our approach toward (1) hunger in our own country; (2) trade; (3) investment; (4) economic assistance; and (5) the military.

8
Hunger USA

Elsie DeFratus was an elderly widow who lived in St. Petersburg, Florida, on less than a hundred dollars a month from Social Security. $15 a week for housing left her 65 cents a day for food. Prices rose. Mrs. DeFratus had less and less to eat and shrank to 76 pounds. On October 3, 1974 she collapsed and died.

"Malnutrition," the coroner said after an autopsy.

Exceptional? To be sure. But Mrs. Defratus was only one of 20 million U.S. citizens estimated by the Senate Select Committee on Nutrition and Human Needs in 1975 to be eligible for food stamps, but not on the program. That means many malnourished people in the United States.

Why Many Are Hungrier

"Over the past three to four years, our nation's needy have become hungrier and poorer," concluded a 1974 report to the Senate committee from the Food Research and Action Center. This, despite the fact that we spend almost $6 billion a year on federal food assistance programs, most of it on food stamps.

Why have so many become hungrier?

One reason is that the food stamp program aims too low. It tries to provide an Economy Plan diet worked out by the U.S. Department of Agriculture. But the government itself admits that few families—perhaps one in ten—can nourish themselves adequately this way. Studies show that even the *least* poor of the poor can barely afford the economy diet. A few years ago the Bureau of Budget said: "The Economy Plan is an emergency diet intended to be used during periods of economic distress. As a permanent diet, the Economy Plan fails to provide sufficient caloric value, although minimum levels of other essential nutrients are sustained." The economy diet assumes sophisticated planning abilities, refrigeration, transportation, and bulk purchases—things that poor families often lack. In effect the food stamp program is designed to alleviate, but not eliminate hunger for those who participate.

Inflation also explains why many U.S. citizens have become hungrier. From December 1970 to March 1974 the cost of the economy diet rose by almost 42 percent; but benefits from the food stamp program increased only 34 percent, and welfare benefits less than 15 percent. Incomes for the working poor, too, climbed more slowly than food prices. Inflation hit poor people hard partly because those above the poverty line have been able to "spend down"—that is, switch from beef to beans. Spending down drives the cost of beans up. But what do people already depending on beans do? They pay more. During the three-year period cited above, the price of porterhouse steaks increased 38 percent, while dried beans went up 256 percent. Spending down for some means eating pet food.

The recession of the mid-1970s added to the number of persons who qualify for, but do not participate in the food stamp program. Why don't they participate? (1) Pride. Pathetically, hunger in our country has become the shame of those who go hungry rather than the shame of us who are well fed. (2) Enrolling often involves traveling long distances several times and waiting for hours. That turns away a lot of the elderly, the working poor and others. (3) With few exceptions, participants have to pay cash in advance for an entire month's supply of stamps; but many hungry people do not have the available cash. (4) County centers are often understaffed and frequently, rather than seeking out eligible persons, do what they can to discourage applications. In 1974 the U.S. Department of Agriculture was blocked by a Federal district Court from returning $280 million in unused food stamp funds. The court said that the Department of Agriculture had spent only 80 thousand dollars nationwide in an outreach effort that is required by law.

These factors help to explain why many hungry and poor people in our country became hungrier and poorer during the first half of the 1970s. But behind these factors lurk more fundamental flaws: chronic unemployment, a welfare system that doesn't work well, wages that keep families of the working poor below the poverty line, and incomes too low to provide bare necessities for many others. All are problems that contribute heavily to the number of hungry persons.

Examples

Some hungry people live in the cities. In June 1974 Mrs. Peggy Ballew of Chicago said that she and her two children received a monthly welfare check of $237—well below the poverty line. $44 of this paid for $112 worth of food stamps—a big help. But even with menus heavy on macaroni and potatoes, the stamps didn't last through the month. What does she tell her children then? "You say, 'I'm sorry, there's nothing to eat.' You talk to them and play with them to get their minds off being hungry."

Mrs. Ballew was testifying before the U.S. Commission on Civil Rights, as it investigated the fact that three-fourths of those receiving public assistance and welfare payments are women. That percentage would drop if more jobs were available, sexual discrimination in hiring reduced, and child care services readily available for mothers who choose to work.

A few years ago a nutritional study of six primary schools on Manhattan's Lower East Side, one of New York's most crowded slums, tested 619 children. The diets of almost three-fourths were rated inadequate. One out of six children had a clinical rating of poor, which showed up in such things as excessive leanness and prominent abdomens. Although the relationship between nutrition and educational achievement has not been fully established, there is little doubt that poor nutrition hinders learning. The children in this nutritional study attended schools in which 80 to 90 percent of those enrolled fall below average reading levels. Poor nutrition for them means a waste of human resources that even in purely economic terms is costly to us.

Many of the U.S. hungry live in rural areas. Harold Cooper, his wife and four children inhabit a tumble-down house on a small patch of land in Georgia. The Coopers rent their acre-and-a-half for $15 a year, their house for $6 a month. They grow some of their own food, but lack refrigeration. Mr. Cooper is in poor health, able to get only occasional odd jobs. Mrs. Cooper needs an operation. The two youngest children are periodically treated for worms, a common problem among youngsters from homes that lack indoor plumbing, and a form of competition for food that contributes heavily to malnutrition worldwide.

Mrs. Cooper explains the family's failure to participate in the food stamp program by complaining about "the way you get treated there." She says that the last ten days of the month the family's diet usually consists of bread, syrup and beans, and sometimes the beans don't hold out. The Cooper children frequently go hungry at school, even though lunches are offered to them at a reduced price of 20 cents each. When all four children go to school, 80 cents is beyond their reach.

The Coopers illustrate the fact that most hungry U.S. citizens are white, although hunger claims a higher *percentage* of black people. The Cooper family also reminds us that hunger is disproportionately concentrated among rural people, especially in the South and in Appalachia.

Many of the rural hungry are migrant farm workers, a group that Edward R. Murrow described in a 1960 CBS documentary, "Harvest of Shame." On that broadcast one of the farmers said, "We used to own our slaves. Now we just rent 'em." Ten years later an NBC documentary, "Migrant," showed that slaves are still being rented. In 1974 migrant workers averaged an annual income of $2,276. They rank among the worst housed, least educated and least protected by law, with neither health insurance nor unemployment insurance and usually no vote.

The vulnerability of migrant farm workers contrasts sharply with the generous subsidies, direct and indirect, that the government has made available to wealthy farmers and large corporate farm enterprises. This favored treatment has driven many small farmholders and farm workers off the land, frequently letting them waste away nearby or in a distant urban slum. Corporations continue to squeeze out family farmers through such advantages as tax shelters (deductions for losses in agriculture) and vertical integration (through contracts with farmers that give companies control of production and marketing and leave the farmer little or no bargaining power). By 1975 support was growing for legislation, introduced in several states and in Congress, to restrict corporate farming and keep farmland in the hands of family farmers.

Among segments of the U.S. population that experience hunger disproportionately, federal statistics point especially to native Americans (Indians). They suffer the most malnutrition, the most illness, the highest infant mortality rate and the lowest life expectancy of any group in the United States. This tragic situation has to be one of the ironies of the nation's history.

Malnourishment, especially during the pre-natal period and the first two years after birth, can lead to mental retardation. It is no accident, then, that three-fourths of the nation's mentally retarded come from areas of urban and rural poverty.

Steps To End Hunger

The fact that the richest nation on earth has within its borders a sizable population of poor and hungry people does no particular honor to us. Not another wealthy, industrialized nation, East or West, tolerates the kind of slums, the persistent unemployment, the lack of medical coverage, or the hunger that still characterizes the United States. Japan, for example, years ago wiped out hunger. All Japanese school children are furnished scientifically balanced lunches with nutrients added. Pregnant mothers and young children get special attention, with a food-supplement program available to all mothers during and after pregnancy. Instead of being relief-oriented, Japan's feeding programs are considered a fundamental investment in the nation. In 1971 citizens of Kobe, Japan, sent a gift of food to Seattle's unemployed Boeing workers, who struggled unsuccessfully for five months to get food assistance from our government.

Most observers believe that China, despite its poverty, has eliminated hunger. But not the United States.

Compared to many other accomplishments, it would be a relatively easy matter to end hunger in this country.

1. *We could establish a national nutrition policy that assures every citizen an adequate diet.* Such a policy would go a long

way toward rescuing the idea of good nutrition from the stigma of welfarism and putting it on a positive basis.

2. *We could improve food assistance.* Japan serves as a useful model, with the food programs mentioned above available to all at no cost, regardless of income. We should offer school lunches, breakfast programs and nutritional help for especially vulnerable persons, such as nursing mothers, infants and the elderly, on the same terms. The food stamp program, too—though properly a stop-gap remedy—could be seen as an opportunity to eradicate hunger and in so doing to safeguard the nation's most precious natural resource: people.

3. *We could adopt a policy of guaranteed employment.* If every employable head-of-family had a job that paid a wage by which he or she could sustain the family above the poverty level, millions of poorly nourished citizens would begin to eat well. Such a policy would benefit the entire nation. We have, side by side, jobless people and rotten housing—an unnecessary contradiction; jobless people and children in schools who need more help—a contradiction; jobless people, when parks and recreational facilities need development, streets need cleaning and people need better health services—all contradictions. There are more than enough things that need to be done. Why can't we let people do them at a decent wage and increase the quality of life for all of us?

4. *Most important of all, we could put a floor of economic decency under every citizen.* Guaranteed work would build part of that floor. With guaranteed work in the picture (or without it, for that matter), is it fair to punish children, old people and handicapped people—those who cannot or should not work—by forcing them to live in poverty? They also need an income that lifts them above this level. That could be done through a negative income tax or a guaranteed income similar to social security. Establishing this floor of economic decency would allow us to phase out the food stamp program and the present inadequate welfare system.

Why, with our wealth, has widespread hunger been permitted to exist in the United States? Part of the answer lies in a long history of devotion to a particular understanding of free enterprise that exalts financial success, while branding the destitute

as moral delinquents. It is a viewpoint that at an earlier period
wanted no government restraints on giant monopolies, but at the
same time demanded that authorities act to outlaw and forcibly
repress the rise of organized labor—all in the name of free enterprise.

The idea that poverty is the result of moral failure has taken
a terrible toll in loss of self-esteem among the poor, and in self-
righteousness among the nonpoor. Both perspectives are so na-
kedly at odds with the Bible that the currency they have gained
even among Christians and Jews is astonishing. Yet people hold
this idea with the best of intentions.

People can change, however. Ernest F. Hollings is a concerned Christian who had seen a lot of poverty, but he believed
that the poor could climb to prosperity all by themselves if they
just tried. "I was a victim of hunger myopia," he admits. "I
can't say that I really saw hunger until I went traveling with a
Catholic nun, Sister Anthony, in January 1968." Though Hollings
was an active Protestant, Sister Anthony thought he meant well
and could learn, so she invited him to visit some families in a
Charleston, South Carolina slum. On a cold and rainy day they
went visiting. According to Hollings:

Before we had gone a block, I was miserable. . . . I began
to understand . . . that hunger was real, and it existed in
hundreds of humans in my own home city. I saw what all
America needs to see. The hungry are not able-bodied men,
sitting around drunk and lazy on welfare. They are children.
They are abandoned women, or the crippled, or the aged.[1]

What makes this story a bit different is that Ernest F. Hollings was (and still is) a U.S. Senator from South Carolina. As
governor of South Carolina he had refused to admit that the
state had a hunger problem. As a U.S. Senator he balked at having a committee of senators investigate hunger in Beaufort
County, South Carolina. But after visiting with some of the
hungry in Charleston, and later in Beaufort County, Hollings
became an ardent supporter of efforts to end hunger in the United States. Senator Hollings concludes his book, *The Case
Against Hunger*, with these words: "America, with its great

wealth and energy, has the ability to wipe out hunger almost overnight. We can, we just haven't."

Domestic and Global Links

Serious as hunger still is for many of our citizens, it cannot be compared either in extent or intensity to hunger for most of the world's poor. The experience of hunger here does, however, underscore some lessons that can be applied even in underdeveloped countries. One is that while feeding hungry people is costly, failure to do so is much more expensive in the long run, because the wreckage of human lives has to be paid for many times over in other ways. Hungry people mean economic stagnation.

Another lesson is that advanced technology and high food production do not in themselves wipe out hunger. Where people are mired in poverty, you may find hunger thriving right along with a food surplus. Therefore the most fundamental and difficult part of the hunger question has to do with remedying the worst features of poverty.

But with so many people hungry in our own country, shouldn't we eliminate hunger here before we try to solve the problem worldwide? This charity-begins-at-home argument appeals, but fails. Pitting domestic hunger against world hunger or vice versa is a great mistake. The two belong together. It is not a case of either/or. We can deal with both; and if we do not deal with both, we will probably deal with neither.

9
Trade: A Hunger Issue

Few people think of trade as a "hunger" issue. However, trade arrangements do more to determine whether millions live or starve than do food assistance and all other forms of aid combined. In 1973 poor countries earned a total of $109 billion in exports. That same year they received $9.4 billion in development assistance—less than 10 percent of their exports. A doubling of aid might be worth less to those countries than a 10 percent improvement in their export earnings.

How Poor Countries Lose Out

So crucial is trade to poor countries that aid, by comparison, has been called a "soft option"—the easy way out. Lester B. Pearson, the late Prime Minister of Canada, once related to a UN official the pressure on a government to prefer that soft option:

> You sit at the Cabinet table [he said in effect] and you tell your colleagues that country X, which we have helped before, has asked for another $Y million. The Minister of Finance, to whom you appeal, agrees that he might perhaps be able to oblige with the necessary funds, but the Minister of Trade intervenes and asks whether it would not be more helpful to assist the exports of country X by allowing duty free entry to Z million shirts. There is an immediate protest from the Minister of Labour, who foresees trouble. You hesitate, and, in the end, you settle for the softer option. You give country X another $Y million, not forgetting that it used some of the previous aid funds to establish a shirt factory for the export trade.[1]

Pearson's example illustrates how poor countries get locked into a losing arrangement. The rules for losing include these five steps:

First, start with a period under colonial rule. Most of today's poor countries are left with systems—transportation, communications, cash crops, industries, and others—that were developed to enrich the ruling country. Political independence does not always prevent those systems from continuing to serve the same purpose.

Second, give raw materials and primary products a low commercial value and let them account for almost 90 percent of the export earnings of poor countries. With these low-cost materials, companies in the rich nations manufacture high-value products—which account for most of their exports to the underdeveloped countries. In 1973 poor nations (not including the major oil exporters) suffered a $12 billion deficit in balance of trade. In 1974 that figure rose to an estimated $20 billion largely as a result of oil (but also grain) price increases.

Third, let the terms of trade (the relationship of export to import prices) turn against the poor countries. Between 1950 and 1970 prices progressively dropped for the raw materials and primary products they sell, in relation to the manufactured products and advanced technology they have to buy from industrialized nations. Despite a stabilizing trend in the 1960s, the Secretariat of the UN Conference on Trade and Development estimated several years ago that worsening terms of trade cost the poor nations $2.5 billion each year. Such losses constitute a huge transfer of resources to the rich nations.

Fourth, let many poor countries depend heavily on a single raw material or a single crop. The price for such exports tends to be low and fluctuates greatly. For example, copper accounts for about 85 percent of Chile's exports, but between April 1974 and March 1975 the price had dropped by more than half. Or consider coffee. When asked a few years ago what his chances of staying in power were, the president of one Central American country replied, "It depends on the price of coffee." He turned out to be a good prophet. The price of coffee fell, and so did the government. The fact that rich countries, as buyers, have often exercised a monopoly-type control of prices over many of these products has not helped the situation.

Fifth, slap tariffs and quotas on manufactured goods coming in from poor countries. In the major trade negotiations of the 1960s (the Kennedy Round) rich nations helped one another by lowering import barriers on products that they manufacture and sell to one another, but largely bypassed farm commodities and the type of labor-intensive goods manufactured by poor nations. As James P. Grant, President of the Overseas Development Council, has stressed, "the tariff structure in force today in the developed countries leads them in effect to charge twice as much duty on the goods they import from the developing world than on the goods they import from one another."[2]

GRAPH #5

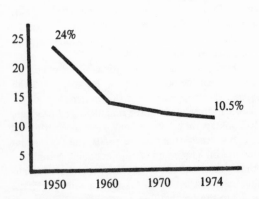

Percentage, by value, of world exports for non-oil-exporting poor countries. Source: UN Conference on Trade and Development.

If poor countries have such handicaps, then the market is not free. It is rigged. Even the lifting of trade restrictions would not make trade fully "free," because countries do not necessarily do business as equals. Rich, powerful countries and companies hold many bargaining advantages.

This helps to explain why the *share* of world exports by non-oil-exporting poor countries shrank from 24 percent in 1950 to 10.5 percent in 1974 (Graph #5). Poor countries pay, by their own exports, for the vast majority of imports, which are vital to their economic growth. The Pearson Commission on International Development reported that "growth rates of individual developing countries since 1950 correlate better with their export performance than with any other single indicator."[3]

For those countries no less than our own, exports mean self-reliance. They mean growth that provides jobs and incomes for people who would otherwise go hungry.

Understandably, poor countries have grown increasingly frustrated for more than a decade by a pattern of trade that seems designed to keep them "hewers of wood and drawers of water" for the rich countries. Out of this frustration poor countries insisted on the establishment of the UN Conference on Trade and Development (UNCTAD) in 1964. This UN agency has repeatedly documented the need for fair trade opportunities, including trade preferences for poor countries and an international monetary system that would do more to support and less to impede development. But their urgings have been brushed aside.

Against this background the oil crisis hit.

The Oil Crisis

The oil crisis that began in October 1973 will affect billions of persons, some living and some not yet born, either locking them more deeply into hunger or helping them out of it. By uniting to control one crucial raw material and forcing its price upward, the Organization of Petroleum Exporting Countries succeeded in calling the rules of the trade system into question, although the outcome of this was far from clear early in 1975.

The initial impact, however, was clear: The quadrupling of oil prices dealt both rich and poor countries a severe blow. The United States paid $17 billion more for oil imports in 1974 than in 1973; but boosted earnings in farm exports offset much of this loss and left our country with a relatively mild trade deficit of $3 billion. In addition "recycled" oil money, returning in the form of investments, helped the U.S. balance of payments. Most other industrialized countries fared worse. Western Europe and Japan together spent about $45 billion more for oil in 1974 and ran a total trade deficit of approximately $37 billion. Hardest hit were countries such as the United Kingdom (Britain), with a trade deficit of $12 billion, and Italy, with a deficit of $8 billion. In each case higher oil prices accounted for most of the deficit.

If the oil crisis hurt the rich nations, it proved disastrous to many of the poorest countries. It adversely affected food production, among other things. The increase that non-oil-producing poor countries paid for oil in 1974 devoured much of their scarce foreign exchange, and their trade deficit of about $20 billion represented a crippling loss (see Graph #6). But $7 billion of that deficit came from the increased cost of *grain* imports since 1972, about $5 billion of that from the United States.

GRAPH #6

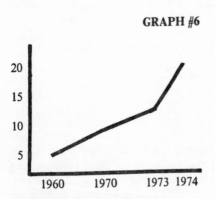

Trade deficit, in billions of dollars, for non-oil-exporting poor countries (with preliminary estimate for 1974). Source: UN Conference on Trade and Development.

Some expected India's economic growth rate, under the burden of oil and grain imports, to fall well below its population growth rate for 1975.

An intriguing question emerges from all of this. Why did poor countries scarcely utter a public word of protest about the oil price hikes that crippled them so? In part, no doubt, because they were angling for assistance from the oil producers, and beginning to get some. But in part, also, for a reason that largely escaped Western notice: *the oil crisis challenged the entire trade structure.* Many from the poor countries saw in the oil crisis, however brutal to them in the short run, a long-range hope for bringing about a new relationship in trade between rich and poor countries.

There were indications that the oil producers might use their leverage to attempt just that. First, oil producing nations committed themselves in 1974 to almost as much development assistance to the poor countries as did all of the traditional aid-giving nations combined. Actual assistance lagged far behind promises, to be sure, with 80 percent of it going to Islamic countries. But that actual assistance represented 1.8 percent of the GNP of aid-giving oil nations—more than five times the .33 percent of GNP contributed by traditional donor nations.

Second, in 1974 President Boumedienne of Algeria played a leading role in the UN Special Assembly on Raw Materials, which declared for a "new international economic order." Third, by the spring of 1975 some oil producing countries appeared ready to bargain for that new order with the industrialized countries. Several oil states were prepared to accept lower oil prices in return, among other things, for higher and more stable prices for basic raw materials that poor countries now export.

Whether or not anything good materializes from this for the poor countries, the oil crisis at least gave *prospect* of doing what years of suffering and rational discourse failed to accomplish: make international trade responsive to the poor countries.

Reducing Trade Barriers

With or without pressure from the major oil producing countries, the United States could seek reforms in world trade that would contribute in a major way toward the ending of hunger.

We could reduce barriers to free trade. Protective tariffs and import quotas work a particular hardship on poor countries, which need to develop markets as they industrialize. For us the issue concerns degrees of abundance; for them it concerns human survival.

The United States charges lower duties to other rich nations than it does to poor nations for manufactured imports. U.S. tariffs escalate so that they are lowest on raw materials, higher on semiprocessed imports, and highest on finished products. The purpose of this is to protect our own labor-intensive industries; but from the standpoint of poor countries, this turns reason inside out. They need, most of all, encouragement to *process* raw materials and to *manufacture* products. Otherwise they are doomed to perpetual subservience: using their raw materials for the rich nations, who reap most of the profits.

Import quotas work a similar disadvantage. According to one observer:

> Our policy has been to support the industrialization of Latin American countries until it reached the point where some of its products were marketable, and then to jam on the brakes. Thus, the ideal aid recipient, from the U.S. point of view, has been a country which can accept development assistance indefinitely, without making any progress.[4]

In one instance the United States loaned money to a Latin American country for a cotton glove manufacturing plant. After the plant was built, a North Carolina firm placed an order for 12 million pair a year. Upon advice of the U.S. Tariff Commission, however, the White House restricted the glove company to a quota of 20,000 pair, thus jamming on the brakes.

Trade barriers hand each of *us* a sizable bill, too, in the form of higher prices, along with the inflationary effect of those prices—a cost to U.S. consumers, by one estimate, of $10 to $15 billion a year, or from $200 to $300 per family. Trade barriers also hurt our export industries. First, by making it hard for poor countries to expand exports, trade barriers sharply curtail their ability to buy from us. Second, they insure that some countries will impose trade restrictions against us or shop elsewhere. That is a penalty of sizable consequence, because over the years our exports have greatly exceeded our imports. The U.S. trade deficit of $3 billion in 1974 was our third calendar-year deficit since 1888.

Protectionism provides a costly solution because in effect it subsidizes our production weaknesses and handicaps our production strengths, a policy that results in *less* real national wealth. A great majority of economists stress that in order to maintain a competitive edge, the United States needs to specialize in areas of comparative advantage, such as higher-technology products.

Economist Paul A. Samuelson, winner of the Nobel Prize, speaks for many of his colleagues when he sees the United States (1) shifting its emphasis from manufacturing to services; (2) accepting as normal an unfavorable balance of trade in consumer goods; (3) paying for this through investment earnings abroad; (4) having a more productive economy as a result; and (5) protecting U.S. workers and industries not with trade barriers but with other guarantees (the topic of the last section of this chapter).

The oil price increases marked a new ball game as far as U.S. trade balances are concerned, and just when other countries are becoming more competitive in some low-wage areas. Already in 1971 industries estimated that imports that year would account for a high portion of U.S. purchases for a number of products:

Home radios, 90%
Black and white TVs, 51%
Shoes, 42%
New cars, 16%
Motorcycles, 96%
Sweaters, 68%

The competition should not be exaggerated, however. In 1974 the United States earned $5.5 billion more in sales to non-oil-exporting *poor* countries than we paid them for imports—a hefty balance. Their competitive ability—and their hungry people—would get a substantial boost if trade barriers were lifted.

Trade Preferences and Stability

Movement toward free trade is not enough. That still leaves poor countries with terms of trade that have steadily worked against them. A few years ago *The Christian Century* described the squeeze this way:

> Caught between rising prices on their industrial imports and falling export prices—and effectively excluded from exporting their own industrial products—Asian, African and Latin American leaders of all ideological hues have been driven toward a Marxist cynicism about the world economy.[5]

That kind of desperation is hard for us to feel. Nevertheless we get an inkling of it by noting the occasional anger of our own trade officials toward Japan. John K. Jessup summarized the reason for that anger in a 1970 *Life* magazine article, "How the Japanese Got So Rich So Fast":

> . . . the Japanese treat us the way prewar Belgians or the Dutch used to treat their colonies. They buy chiefly our raw materials—lumber, cotton, wheat, coal, soybeans—and sell us a wide range of high-technology, high-profit manufactured goods. If this trend continues, the U.S. trade deficit with Japan could be $4 billion by 1973.[6]

As it turned out, we reached the $4 billion trade deficit with Japan in 1972. But the point worth noting is that what Jessup described is exactly the position the poor countries find themselves in *vis-à-vis* the United States—only without the resources to make up for it in other ways or the leverage to fight back.

Part of the answer lies in *trade preferences* for the poorest countries. The United States could gradually eliminate tariffs on imports from those countries, while still allowing them to protect their infant industries. The Common Market countries of Europe have moved in that direction. Although the United States has endorsed the principle of trade preferences, it has yet to act on that principle. The Trade Act of 1974 authorizes the President to negotiate trade preferences, if he so chooses—but it also authorizes him to impose restrictions.

Stability in trade arrangements is also essential. In 1975 Common Market countries signed with 46 former European colonies an agreement to set up a $450 million stabilization fund for 12 basic commodities imported, mostly duty-free, from the forty-six. This will provide them with a type of guarantee roughly similar to government target prices that assure U.S. farmers at least a minimal return on some key farm commodities.

Stability goes beyond prices and primary commodities, however. Poor countries must know that if they develop a successful industry it will not be put out of business with one stroke of a pen by the President of the United States through an arbitrary shift in tariffs or quotas. Uncertainty about U.S. trade policies often discourages those with wealth in poor countries from investing in domestic enterprises. If you had $500,000 and you lived in a developing country, would you invest it there or put the money in a Swiss or North American bank? Frequently we encourage the wrong answer.

In some cases international agreements on production, as well as prices, could give poor countries a fairer chance. According to historian J. H. Parry, the Virginia colony was saved from economic ruin and allowed to achieve modest wealth when England agreed to destroy its own tobacco acreage and give the Virginia planters a monopoly on this crop. In the same spirit, adjustments on the part of rich nations today could help to achieve long-range benefits for everyone.

International agreements are also needed in order to prevent countries from suddenly withholding essential exports. The oil embargo of 1973 and U.S. soybean and fertilizer embargoes that same year provide examples of actions that should be avoided.

The use of price agreements and tariff preferences qualifies but does not set aside the goal of free trade. Free trade would still apply to trading equals and affect the great majority of exports and imports. By allowing poor countries temporary advantages, however, this approach makes free trade a less absolute goal than fair trade, although it would move the world toward both. By the same token of fairness, countries like our own need to proceed gradually in order to cushion themselves against a sudden influx of products from abroad, and to give their economies time to adjust.

Fair trade and free trade are achievable goals—if we have

committed leadership. In March 1972 the *Journal of Commerce* observed—approvingly:

> The administration has stalled on its contribution to the International Development Association [the World Bank's soft loan division]. It doesn't want any special allocation of . . . special drawing rights to the LDCs [less developed countries] in excess of their normal quotas. It won't consider preferential tariffs for the time being. It doesn't want to see the LDCs ordering half or more of their trade to be routed in their own ships. And it seems in no hurry to make the monetary adjustments that could make the U.S. market more lucrative for overseas commodity exports.
>
> In other words, just about every major proposal put forth in the interests of protecting the LDCs from further deterioration in their terms of trade is drawing a negative reaction in Washington. [7]

The United States can do better than that.

Adjustments at Home

A generous trade policy should be coupled with a thorough adjustment program at home. Labor is rightly concerned about the loss of jobs in industries that face a new competitive challenge from abroad. Business and farm sectors also have serious concerns. Industries that suffer because of foreign imports should readily qualify for low-interest, government-guaranteed loans so that they can become competitive again or move into other areas of production. A U.S. farm program should encourage the family farmer and stimulate world food production, while it discourages competition with developing nations, and that may require adjustments from time to time. The entire nation should share the burden, just as it shares the benefits, of trade reform.

Some of labor's anxiety centers on the exporting of jobs by U.S. firms that transfer their capital and technology to an underdeveloped country, where an affiliate can turn out products at wages that range up to ten times lower than in the United States. But if we are to reap the benefits of rationalizing the world's production and distribution, then we must also rationalize production and distribution in the United States so that workers in adversely affected industries can turn to acceptable alternatives.

A key part of the answer is to guarantee a job to all U.S. citizens, in the private sector insofar as possible, but with the government as the employer of last resort. The entire society then assumes the adjustment burden—and the entire society will benefit from a reduction in crime, welfare costs and other things that plague us partly because of our high unemployment. In addition, we can do more work on long neglected needs, such as rebuilding cities and improving our environment, our schools and our health services.

A companion measure mentioned in the previous chapter would provide a floor of economic decency under each U.S. citizen. A U.S. policy of guaranteed work, together with a guaranteed economic floor for all citizens, is important to the poor countries because its adoption would make possible greater support of a generous trade program. Without such an approach U.S. workers, and those aspiring to work, will constantly fear that gains abroad may eliminate jobs. In this way the nation now generates internal pressure for frustrating the aspirations of hungry people around the globe.

With policies of guaranteed employment, of income insurance, of adjustment assistance when needed to the family farmer, and of low-interest loans to companies hurt by changing patterns of trade, various sectors of our economy could play key roles in supporting the extension of trade opportunities to poor countries.

10
The Role of
Investment Abroad

When a rich man does business with a poor man, the rich man usually has an advantage, so their agreement tends to be weighted in the rich man's favor. If a poor man needs a job, he may (or may not) have to take what he can get on the rich man's terms. As we have seen in the case of trade, dealings between rich and poor persons often have their counterpart in dealings between rich and poor nations. What is said about trade applies also to corporate investment abroad: It can either assist in the struggle against hunger, or it can do the opposite.

Like trade, international investment is not seen by the public as a hunger issue, but does much to determine who eats well and who dies. Poor countries depend partly on foreign investments for the capital and technology that growing economies require. Without growing economies their people have little hope of escaping hunger.

To cite one critical example, jobs are at stake. Today in the poor countries unemployment is soaring. People enter the job market not only in unprecedented numbers, but at a *rate* about five times faster than that which today's rich countries usually experienced when they were at comparable stages of development. No wonder, then, that in an *Indicative World Plan* the UN Food and Agriculture Organization calls the problem of employment "far more intractable than that of food supply" in reducing world hunger. Poor countries need foreign investments to generate jobs.

Investment without Empire

If both rich and poor countries are to benefit economically from the comparative advantages of each other, that will happen not only through more enlightened trade policies, but through enlightened investment practices as well. Poor countries need capital and technology; and multinational corporations, together with banks, have proven to be astonishingly effective in achieving that transfer.

The question is: Can companies build investments abroad without building economic empires that do in their own way what the old colonial empires used to do: take advantage of local populations in order to enrich themselves? The question is not simply one of profit-making, without which the transfers would not occur; rather it has to do with *excessive* profits, *control*, and *the shape development takes in a country*. In this connection a number of concerns emerge:

1. *Bigness.* The sheer size of the multinational corporations and the extent of their global reach prompt concern. In 1972, with nations and corporations ranked together on the basis of their total production, 42 of the top hundred were companies, 20 of them (generally the larger ones) headquartered in the United States. In 1970 production by multinationals accounted for one-sixth of the world's total, including 40 percent of the world's *industrial* production, and that percentage is increasing. Some think that multinational corporations will soon control most of the world's manufacturing assets. In any case, the trend is toward additional concentration. U.S. direct investments abroad climbed from $32 billion in 1960 to $107 billion in 1973 ($28 billion of it in poor countries). In 1973 these investments returned profits of $17.5 billion, one-third of it from poor countries. One-fourth of U.S. corporate profits and one-half of U.S. industrial profits come from overseas.

2. *Accountability.* "The past two decades have witnessed an enormous growth of corporate power at the global level without a corresponding growth of public accountability," writes Lester R. Brown in *World Without Borders*. Too often companies have taken undue advantage of cheap raw materials, cheap labor and various tax havens in order to maximize profits. Accounting

rigged to send profits to company affiliates in countries with little or no taxation, and price manipulation are among the abuses.

3. *Control.* By dominating strategic industries or key sectors
of the economy, companies may exercise control far out of proportion to the size of their holdings, which in themselves may be
extensive. Even rich countries sometimes protest. In the mid-
1960s Europeans began to complain bitterly that U.S. corporations were turning their countries into economic colonies. By
consolidating efforts, however, Europe, with its advanced technology and strong economies stood well against this threat. To a
lesser extent so has Canada, even though most of its industry is
U.S.-owned and controlled. Ironically, increased investments in
this country by major oil producers gives some of our own citizens the jitters. Although total private foreign investments in the
United States were about one-fifth of private U.S. investments
abroad early in 1975, and amounted to perhaps 2 percent of total
private investment in this country, legislation had been introduced in Congress asking for safeguards.

By contrast, consider poor countries with small, weak economies. The impact there is far greater. In 1970 Gunnar Myrdal
estimated regarding Latin America that

> . . . directly or indirectly, through joint enterprises and
> other arrangements, United States corporations now control
> or decisively influence between 70 and 90 percent of the
> raw-material resources of Latin America, and probably
> more than half of its modern manufacturing industry, bank-
> ing, commerce, and foreign trade, as well as much of its
> public utilities.[1]

Another cause for alarm in Latin America is growing U.S. do-
minance in the communications media, which often promote
consumer tastes that militate against development needs. You
can understand the feeling of people in many poor countries that
they are being swallowed up.

4. *Misdevelopment.* Is a new Sears, Roebuck store or an
auto plant what a poor country needs? Perhaps, but perhaps not.
Countries often fail to reach their hungry citizens with development programs. Resources may be concentrated on a small

urban population and neglect agriculture, or provide a growing middle class with potato chips and barbie dolls, but bypass the poor. Sometimes this is exactly what leaders of poor countries want, but often it happens against their will. Desperate to provide jobs and opportunities to their people, but lacking the capital and management skills to develop modern industries, those countries may have to attract foreign companies by offering generous inducements, such as low interest loans, over-valued exchange rates or lavish tax concessions. Sometimes those industries provide relatively few jobs for the capital invested, but host countries may feel that a few jobs are better than none, or be lured by the hope—often disappointed—of earning much foreign exchange.

Facing massive poverty and unemployment with few resources of their own puts great pressure on poor countries to gamble on this approach. For their part, multinational companies have big bargaining chips and shop around for the best incentives, and this may push countries down the wrong road.

If too much profit goes back to the investing companies and if local people are not taught skills and brought into managerial positions, far from spreading economic benefits, such enterprises discourage national industries. More than occasionally, national industries sell out to foreign companies. This happens in some cases because banks in poor countries may prefer to loan money to the multinationals rather than to local businessmen or farmers, giving giant firms another competitive advantage.

5. *Political Influence and Corruption.* The attempt by ITT covertly to prevent Salvador Allende from becoming President of Chile, and later to undermine his administration, is an extreme and fortunately uncommon instance of political intervention. But there are many less dramatic examples of companies seeking to improperly influence government policies in host countries. Bribery on the part of U.S. firms abroad (a tax deductible item!) also constitutes abuse of power.

Often as important is the effect that U.S.-based companies can have on our own policy toward the countries in which they operate. Because change often shakes stability and creates an atmosphere less conducive to making profits, U.S. business interests tend to discourage our government from favoring needed reforms. This influence helped to scuttle the Alliance for Progress, as investments were talked up and reforms talked down, and has also encouraged the United States to back repressive governments. Hindering civil liberties in this way cultivates for U.S. business a reputation that contradicts the freedom it espouses at home.

This quest by business for stability-without-reform unfortunately dovetails with the State Department's tendency to give stability abroad a higher rating than democracy. Stability is a condition to be greatly desired. But an overriding preference for stability, combined with investment practices that tend to hinder rather than assist the poor, may cause Western industrialists to play into the hands of both communist and right-wing extremists who need above all to convince people that gradualism through democracy offers no hope for improvement.

The Profit Motive

The above concerns raise the question: Are business ventures abroad compatible with the requirements of development in the poor nations? Not necessarily. Private enterprise thrives on the profit motive. Companies go to unfamiliar lands, where the risks and difficulties tend to be abnormal, because they expect to make a return on their investment great enough to offset possible disadvantages. This applies pressure for a "quick kill" on profits, or for excessive long-range returns, a situation that often counteracts healthy growth in those countries. Company representatives may have no idea, or a warped idea, of a country's own development plans and, if so, decisions will reflect this. Evil intent is not a prerequisite.

On the other hand the list of pitfalls does not lead to the conclusion that U.S. business investments are always at loggerheads with the needs of poor countries. Rather it leads us away from the assumption that such ventures *automatically* contribute to healthy development and require no restraints. Many of them do contribute to development; many do not. Just as British capital helped to finance industrial growth in the United States during the last century, so the capital and skills that Western firms now bring to poor countries can be invaluable, *provided they fulfill real development needs*. That is a less brash, less arrogant, and perhaps even a less profitable role than the one we are accustomed to. It reflects the real world with painful, stubborn problems, not a tidy, make-believe world whose needs always coincide with our ambitions. But it is a role that can work out to the mutual advantage of both company and underdeveloped country. The model should be that of private enterprise helping to service development for a reasonable return.

Accountability

Two recent UN reports on multinational corporations and a study by a subcommittee of the U.S. Senate, along with a number of articles and books, have encouraged the idea of making multinational companies accountable. Because the issue is complex and controversial, and information still sketchy, the process of accountability will develop gradually.

A 1974 UN report on multinationals by the Group of Eminent Persons recommended that the UN Economic and Social Council (ECOSOC) consider the subject on a regular basis, assisted by a Commission on Transnational Corporations, now in operation. The Commission was asked to "evolve a set of recommendations which, taken together, would represent a code of conduct for governments and multinational corporations to be considered and adopted by the Economic and Social Council," and to "explore the possibility of concluding a general agreement on multinational corporations, enforceable by appropriate machinery, to which participating countries would adhere by means of an international treaty."

Primary responsibility for making companies accountable still depends and may always depend on individual governments. Toward that end ECOSOC has established an Information and Research Center on Transnational Corporations that, among other things, helps poor countries improve their capacity to negotiate with corporations.

Nationalization

One option that poor countries seem certain to exercise from time to time is that of nationalizing foreign-owned industries. The nationalization of Chile's copper mines is a case in point. Chile has the world's largest reserve of copper. It is of exceptionally high grade, and it accounts for most of Chile's export earnings. If political consensus is taken as a reflection of popular opinion, then most Chileans—not only socialists—considered the ownership of Chilean copper mines by U.S. companies as a form of outside control no longer acceptable.

Because the U.S. companies had their own processing firms, the government of Chile argued in 1971, they sold copper to themselves at a price well below the world market. The companies made profits alleged by the government—and denied by the companies—to be excessive.

When the Chilean government announced the nationalization of the copper industry, President Allende stressed that Chile was buying the copper industry, not confiscating it. But he insisted that excessive profits be taken into account in determining a fair price. Subsequently the government announced that such profits far exceeded the value of the copper mines and that, therefore, no compensation would be forthcoming. After Allende's overthrow the new military government agreed to compensate the companies. It did not offer to return them, however, because nationalization had been supported by all major parties in Chile before Allende's election.

Other Options

In an essay, *How To Divest in Latin America and Why*, Albert O. Hirschman suggested inducing new investments by permitting higher initial profits, but with ownership automatically reverting to nationals after a specified number of years. The suggestion includes training nationals in management and technical skills. For existing foreign-owned industries, Hirschman favors an arrangement that permits local investors—preferably white- and blue-collar workers, especially those working in companies

—to buy up those industries. He proposes an Inter-American Divestment Corporation which could assist in this by acquiring ownership until local purchasers are found. An approach along this line could gain favor among foreign investors if pressures against them mount.

Along more conventional lines and in the area of food production, the UN Food and Agriculture Organization has served as an "honest broker" for companies and countries through its Industrial Cooperative Program. The ICP tries to match companies and countries. Governments may pass along their food problems to the ICP, which notifies company members and, if a government requests it, may send a survey team to study possibilities. The ICP is regarded as a neutral party willing to advise against projects that would give any company a lopsided advantage. Investments undertaken with ICP help include joint ownership between company and country, and national ownership with a corporation contracted to manage the enterprise.

Perhaps, in the future, ownership will be increasingly closed to foreigners, and U.S. firms will export by contract their management and technical skills to the poor countries. Whatever the formulas, it should be possible for multinational firms and poor countries to work out investment agreements that, by serving authentic development needs, contribute to the reduction of hunger.

11
Foreign Aid:
A Case for Reform

"Give a man a fish and you feed him for a day. Teach him how to fish and you feed him for a lifetime."

This oft-repeated Chinese proverb would be easy to ridicule. Look, for example, at the decline in the world's fish-catch and the capital-intensive fishing methods that bring most of that catch to the already well fed rather than to the hungry. Or visit regions where people go hungry and see if they are near water swarming with fish, lacking only someone who can show them how to throw in a line. Still, the proverb is useful because it affirms the importance of self-reliance. Assistance should not make people depend permanently on handouts, but enable them to work their own way out of hunger and poverty.

The Role of Assistance

Because the self-help approach to assistance is crucial, the fact needs emphasis that only a small part of new investment in poor countries comes from the rich nations. About 85 percent comes from their own savings. The remainder consists mainly of private foreign investment and of loans rather than grants. Food aid is no exception. Despite the public image India has of living off massive shipments of free food, during recent difficult years India imported 4 to 7 percent of its grain, and most of that was bought on the world market at commercial rates. Little went as a direct gift.

Generous help from the outside has, however, almost always been necessary for *rapid* growth. Although rapid growth does not ensure proper development, proper development must take place rapidly because of increased hunger, unemployment and population. Apart from a few oil-rich countries, the only rapidly developing noncommunist nations are those that have received extraordinary aid. Assistance is only a small part of the overall development picture, but it plays a key role.

Some assistance is wasted, of course. Food can rot on docks. Inept or corrupt officials may siphon off aid. Assistance needs—and usually gets—constant watchdogging because these problems are not imaginary. They are often exaggerated, however, and do not nullify the vital contribution that assistance makes. After both world wars much assistance that went from this country to Europe entered the black market; yet these efforts prevented countless deaths and much suffering and helped people get on their feet. The same is true today.

"Money is not the answer," people frequently say. They are right in the sense that successful development requires primarily other inputs, apart from which money won't help much. Each country must use its own resources, chiefly abundant labor. But we cannot escape the fact that even a labor-intensive approach requires substantial capital. A simple thing like the use of fertilizer means that poor farmers need access to credit at reasonable rates of interest, and that presupposes a reserve of capital. It may also suggest the desirability of establishing a fertilizer industry, but that, too, has to be financed. When you add the cost of other improvements such as pest control, tools and building materials, the need for money becomes obvious. Determination and muscle are not enough. Furthermore grassroots leaders should spread throughout the countryside and work with the rural population in teaching a wide variety of skills. The cost of this may be modest in terms of eventual growth, but the cost cannot be wished away.

Food-for-work projects illustrate this further. Under these projects people are paid with food rather than money to do such work as digging irrigation canals or building roads, clinics, schools and storage facilities. Better nourishment is one objective of this program—not surprising when you remember that most hungry people are rural dwellers. Agriculturalist René Dumont says of one area in India that, with extra food rations to give them needed energy, the workers could have dredged irrigation reservoirs during the off season and prepared rich fields that would have produced two harvest instead of one each year. Such programs require capital in the form of food and the nonlabor costs of construction. When assistance for them drops, as it did when food prices soared, food-for-work projects get cut back. It doesn't help to say, "Money is not the answer."

In November 1974 the World Food Conference asked that an International Fund for Agricultural Development be established, with the goal of increasing assistance for rural development from about $1.5 billion a year to $5 billion annually by 1980. That $5 billion would be only a part of the $18 to $20 billion needed, so three-fourths of the capital for rural development has to come from the poor countries themselves.

The World Bank and a number of countries began responding soon to the appeal of the World Food Conference. But action by the U.S. Congress, cutting back assistance for agricultural development and nutrition by $246 million from an amount previously authorized for fiscal year 1975, clearly moved in the opposite direction.

Outside assistance can provide the difference between hunger and health, between stagnation and development. It is a matter of some consequence, then, that, measured as a percentage of rich countries' total income, as well as in value to poor countries, official development assistance has steadily dropped for more than a decade. In dollar terms, donor nations increased their assistance by 9 percent between 1972 and 1973 to a record figure of $9.4 billion. But if changes in exchange rates and price increases are taken into account, it *fell* by 6 percent. Measured in assistance per person living in poor countries, development aid declined in real terms by 30 percent from 1963 to 1973. Further, in 1974 poor countries paid back $8.4 billion in debt retirement to donor nations—almost as much as they received in new assistance.

Add to this the $20 billion trade deficit of non-oil-exporting poor countries for 1974, and *the rich nations* become net recipients of money from the poor ones. This Scrooge-like arrangement ignores the reality of world hunger and the benefits that development could confer on the entire world.

Why Assistance Has Declined

If the purpose of U.S. economic assistance is to help people out of hunger and poverty, then it falls far short of the mark. One reason for this failure is that *aid to the poor countries, never sufficient to begin with, began dropping in the 1960s*. To say that *insufficient* aid is a cause of failure pays indirect tribute to its considerable accomplishments, without which the world would be much worse today.

Development aid is a relatively new idea. After World War II massive private efforts by U.S. citizens and agencies, together with the help of our government, brought food and clothing to many destitute Europeans. But it soon became apparent that the nations of Europe could not rise quickly from the ashes and rebuild themselves. Spurred by this and by fear of Soviet communism, in 1947 the United States proposed a European Recovery Program (the Marshall Plan). By 1952 the United States had poured into Western Europe $23 billion (about $47 billion in 1975 dollars) in official development assistance, not counting military aid or private assistance. Western Europe seemed well on the way toward a dramatic recovery.

In his 1949 inaugural address, President Truman proposed "a bold new program for making the benefits of our scientific advances and industrial progress available for the improvement and growth of underdeveloped areas." Truman suggested that what began for Europe now be extended to the poor nations.

By far the greatest concentration of our aid went to Western Europe. During the four-year period from 1949 to 1952 the United States sent more than $12 billion as outright grants (aside from loans and private help) to Western Europe in the form of official development assistance. By comparison we gave all of Latin America $5 billion in such grants spread over 25 years from 1946 to 1970. During the same 25-year period development grants to all poor countries totalled $40 billion, but $15 billion of that was concentrated in a few countries (Greece, Turkey, Taiwan, Indochina and South Korea) with acute security needs but only 5 percent of the population of all poor countries. To the other 95 percent we allotted roughly $1 billion a year in development grants. On a per capita basis Europe received a concentration of aid several dozen times that of most poor countries.

Why this imbalance? And why has even this assistance tapered off?

For one reason, the people of Europe had millions of close relatives in this country, and countless other U.S. citizens still remembered their European origins. As a result, in virtually every congressional district a powerful grassroots lobby promoted the Marshall Plan. If your member of Congress made speeches about assisting people abroad, he received cheers. He was on the side of the angels and—possibly as important to him —the voters.

In addition, results of our aid to Europe were immediate and dramatic. Countries there already had advanced technology, education, skills and many facilities. They needed a boost to get their disrupted economies going again. But poor countries have none of these advantages. We spread aid to them exceedingly thin by comparison. Not surprisingly, the results disappointed the U.S. public.

Criticism from abroad soured some aid supporters, who felt that recipients were not sufficiently grateful. In recent years the United States and a majority of poor countries have frequently lined up on different sides at the United Nations, and this has corroded support for assistance. "Why should we help them if they oppose us?" people sometimes say.

Aid also tapered off because U.S. taxpayers still think the United States plays the role of Santa Claus in the world. It does not. People have a greatly exaggerated idea of how much this country spends on development assistance. In 1974 the United States ranked 14th among 17 nations that make up the Development Assistance Committee (see Graph #7), when aid was measured as a percentage of national production, and our share is steadily dropping. In 1949, 3 percent of our Gross National Product went to Europe as assistance. By 1975 the figure for U.S. aid to poor countries did not reach *one-tenth* of that percentage of our GNP.

The 1975 foreign assistance bill enacted by Congress totaled $3.67 billion. But almost $2 billion of that was either direct military aid or military-related in the form of security supporting assistance and postwar reconstruction. If you exclude also items

GRAPH #7

1974 Assistance as Percentage of GNP

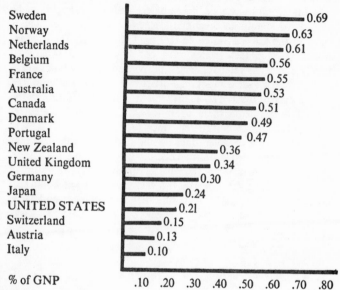

Country	% of GNP
Sweden	0.69
Norway	0.63
Netherlands	0.61
Belgium	0.56
France	0.55
Australia	0.53
Canada	0.51
Denmark	0.49
Portugal	0.47
New Zealand	0.36
United Kingdom	0.34
Germany	0.30
Japan	0.24
UNITED STATES	0.21
Switzerland	0.15
Austria	0.13
Italy	0.10

% of GNP   .10 .20 .30 .40 .50 .60 .70 .80

Estimate of official development assistance. Source: Organization for Economic Cooperation and Development.

such as aid to Cuban refugees in the United States and aid to U.S. schools and hospitals abroad, total U.S. bilateral and multilateral development assistance came to about $1.5 billion. *Thus real U.S. development assistance for 1975 amounted to no more than one-tenth of 1 percent of our GNP, a cost to each citizen of less than two cents a day.*

Those figures do not include U.S. food assistance, which totaled an additional $1.3 billion in 1975. However, three-fourths of that went in the form of low-interest loans to be repaid; and 30 percent of our food aid was designated for countries in which U.S. political and security considerations were uppermost. Because most U.S. food assistance requires repayments, it yields "a substantial balance of payments benefit to the United States," according to our government, which reported a net inflow from food assistance of $174 million for 1974.

Like food assistance, development assistance should not be considered simply an economic loss. Much of that assistance is spent in the United States. In fact the U.S. Agency for International Development (which runs our bilateral aid programs) points out: "The relatively small proportion of AID funds spent overseas each year is more than offset by receipts of interest and repayments on past AID loans, resulting in a net inflow to the United States from these operations." The United States received $752 million in AID repayments for 1974.

While these considerations do not detract from the fact that there is a real flowing out of U.S. resources through assistance, it does show that we get sizable compensations. An estimate applied to 1971 by the Overseas Development Council would still hold: "Since we have a high rate of unemployment and large unused productive capacity, the economic cost of aid to us was probably near zero."[1]

A Purpose Gone Astray

If U.S. assistance does not adequately help people out of hunger and poverty because it has been too limited, there is another reason why it flounders: *The purpose of spurring development has been sidetracked and aid has been promoted instead for other purposes, chiefly as a tool for stopping communism.* The "other purposes," far from hidden, have been openly used in order to win public support and get appropriations through Congress. Some argue that without these motivations U.S. assistance would have diminished even more. Without leadership, probably so. But in recent years foreign assistance has been increasingly abandoned by humanitarians, within and outside of Congress, who believe that aid has become captive to a mistaken understanding of this nation's role in the world.

What "other purposes" have steered it askew?

Propping up U.S. agriculture played a major part in U.S.

food assistance (the Food for Peace Program). Congress enacted Public Law 480 in 1954 to dispose of vast food surpluses. Although the purpose of combating hunger was mentioned in P.L. 480, that law listed a prior objective: "to develop and expand export markets for United States agricultural commodities." So cotton and tobacco are also part of the Food for Peace program. P.L. 480 was a great boon to hungry people abroad, but it also helped us enormously. And when worldwide grain shortages occurred, we sold the surpluses at inflated prices and reduced our food assistance.

Providing markets for U.S. business has also influenced foreign assistance. Contrary to the impression that recipient nations shop around, almost all U.S. assistance funds used to purchase products are spent in the United States. Bilateral aid is typically tied to such purchases. In 1971 when the foreign aid bill was temporarily scuttled, *The Wall Street Journal* headlined a story: "U.S. Firms Push To Get Aid Bill Resurrected; The Stakes: About $1 Billion in Annual Sales."

The main way, however, in which development assistance got sidetracked was for the purpose of combating communism. In part this was deliberate, in part unforeseen. The Marshall Plan followed on the heels of the Truman Doctrine, which declared support for free people resisting internal or external aggression and was aimed immediately at communist threats within Greece and Turkey. So the Cold War played a prominent role even in the European Recovery Program.

Then in 1950, just 20 days after Congress enacted Truman's Point Four Program for aid to poor countries, the Korean War broke out. The impact was stunning. Defense against communism suddenly dominated the entire aid program. We concentrated our assistance in countries where security considerations were uppermost. Until 1970 tiny Taiwan got as much in economic grants as did India. Countries with autocratic and corrupt governments that stood militantly against communism—and often against social reforms as well—were frequently lavished with aid, while neutral countries got comparatively little.

After the food shortage came, Food for Peace became increasingly pressed into the service of war. In 1974 most of our food assistance went to Indochina, where it was sold on the open market to generate money to pay troops and to help faltering war economies.

Or consider the Alliance for Progress. From 1946 until President Kennedy initiated the Alliance in 1961, our development grants to all of Latin America totaled less than $1.2 billion (compared to $1.6 billion for Taiwan during the same period). The Alliance was sold to Congress as a way of preventing Castro from exporting his revolution to other Latin countries. When that danger receded, so did interest in the Alliance. President Kennedy had made clear that success of the Alliance depended on democratic social reforms taking place. Soon after Kennedy's death, President Johnson put Thomas C. Mann in charge of the Alliance. Mann stressed protection of U.S. business investments and neutrality on social reforms. Reforms faded and the Alliance became just another underfunded, unimaginative aid program.

The Rockefeller report in 1969 continued to view structural change in Latin America as a threat against which the United States must strengthen the hand of anticommunist rulers with increased military aid. Consistent with this, the United States withheld aid from Allende's government in Chile, assisted in his overthrow, and promptly restored assistance to the new military dictatorship.

The Alliance had lost its way. But without adequate leadership or a discerning public, so to a large extent had the entire U.S. foreign assistance program.

Needed Reforms

These reforms are urgently needed:

1. *The separation of development assistance from military assistance.* These two forms of aid can be clearly divorced. Congress should consider them separately, and the public should not be misled by seeing them lumped together. In addition, "security supporting assistance"—aid in which military considerations are uppermost—should be counted as military aid. Such aid may be needed, but it should not be confused with humanitarian assistance. Even postwar reconstruction in Indochina, though it may deserve high priority, should be considered part of the cost of the war.

2. *The separation of development assistance from political considerations.* Complete separation is impossible, but we could eliminate the worst abuses. The 1970 report of the Presidential Task Force on International Development warned: "This country should not look for gratitude or votes, or any specific short-term foreign policy gains from our participation in international development."

3. *A fair count on development aid.* Loans should not get the same value as grants. Either repayments on previous aid loans should be subtracted from the assistance total, or the loans should be counted on the basis of special terms of credit involved. For example the World Bank estimated in 1975 that at 4.5 percent interest, $1 billion in long-term loans would require a subsidy of $200 million. If loans were counted this way, and military and political assistance handled separately, the public would, for the first time, get a true—and surprising—picture of our assistance to hungry, impoverished people.

4. *A new set of standards on the basis of which assistance can be determined.* These standards should, if possible, be established by international agreement among aid-giving and aid-receiving nations. The standards would include: (a) need; (b) evidence that development is occurring among the masses of poor people; (c) evidence of basic reforms, such as land reform, tax reform, and anticorruption measures, in order to reduce the disparity between rich and poor within a country; (d) efforts to secure human rights; and (e) de-emphasis on military spending. The way a country measured up to these standards would determine how much or how little assistance it could get.

The standards provide a mere sketch. Negotiation and implementation of them would be difficult, but within reach. They could be carried out on a bilateral basis, failing wider agreement; but poor countries might be surprisingly ready to help initiate such an agreement. It would give leaders leverage to do what some of them may want, but fear to do for domestic political reasons.

For example, two decades ago, when Illinois had a serious teacher shortage, some of the state's most highly qualified teachers were unable to get jobs because they were black. The legislature enacted a law saying that before a school could receive state aid, it had to show that it had not discriminated racially in the employment of teachers. Suddenly many school superintendents found it both desirable—and politically acceptable to their school boards—to change employment practices. The motivation may not have been ideal, but the result was good. In a similar way, the carrot of assistance can help countries adopt better development practices.

5. *The channeling of development assistance primarily through international agencies.* President Truman's Point Four proposal urged that assistance "be a cooperative enterprise in which all nations work together through the United Nations and its specialized agencies whenever practicable." These agencies are not perfect instruments, but use of them would move us away from the criticism that we are trying to hold countries politically hostage.

6. *The channeling of more assistance through church and other voluntary agencies.* In general these agencies have excellent records for sensitivity to different cultures and for meeting human needs on a person-to-person level.

7. *Increased assistance for development among the rural poor, along the lines suggested by the World Food Conference.* The additional $3.5 billion a year sought from donor nations for rural development represents about one-seventieth of global military spending. The $3.5 billion sum is also small compared to the $9 billion *increase* requested by the Administration for U.S. defense spending in 1976. One area that deserves much stronger support is *agricultural research*, including research institutes emphasizing tropical agriculture. Directly related to the development of tropical agriculture is tropical disease, global expenditures for which in 1974 were less than $25 million, compared to about $400 million spent on cancer research alone in the United States that same year.

8. *Increased food assistance, emphasizing grants rather than loans, as part of U.S. participation in a world food reserve program.* The U.S. response should reflect its position as exporter of most of the world's grain, as well as the disproportionate amount it earns (see Chapter 1) in grain sales to poor countries. A tithe (10 percent) of U.S. exports could be set aside for food assistance. The global target set by the World Food Conference is 10 million tons a year until a 60 million ton reserve has been

achieved. In addition U.S. food aid should be put on a strictly humanitarian basis.

9. *Adoption of 1 percent of GNP as the target for development assistance.* The United States can lead the way in supporting assistance for development. The 1 percent target, suggested by the (Pearson) Commission on International Development, was widely accepted in the late 1960s as a reasonable goal. One percent of GNP is a modest target, but, if counted honestly, substantial.

Following the pattern of Sweden, the United States might pledge to raise its assistance by *one-tenth* of 1 percent each year until the full goal has been reached. This gradual approach could be a way of committing the nation, meanwhile, to eliminate hunger and much of the poverty within our own borders. And it would place assistance on a more sure footing than annual political whims allow.

Can we afford to do it? The question should be: Can we afford not to? A home owner can "save" by not painting his house, not patching his roof, or not fixing a broken furnace. In a similar way we can "save" money by not spending it on urgent world needs, but the real cost of such thrift should be tallied in terms of human suffering.

Fourteen days before he died, President Kennedy addressed the Protestant Council of the City of New York and urged church leaders to support foreign aid. He deplored the fact that it had dropped to a mere 4 percent of the national budget (it is less than 1 percent now) and added, "I do not want it said of us what T. S. Eliot said of others some years ago:

'Here were decent godless people:
Their only monument the asphalt road
And a thousand lost golf balls.' "

Perhaps more to the point, what if the final judgment of history's Lord on Christians in the earth's richest nation is simply, "I was hungry, but you would not feed me"?

12
Let Them Eat Missiles

By an excessive reliance on military power the United States has undermined its capacity to reduce world hunger. As long as the politics of power rather than the politics of justice dominates our thinking, we will do little to assist countries overwhelmed by poverty.

This nation's defense requirements are admittedly enormous and costly. Given the stance of present Soviet leadership, acknowledging the need for reasonable power-balancing, and taking into account the soaring costs of both nuclear and nonnuclear technology, our military spending will be high. But we have exceeded the limits of reason. We depend too much on raw power and pay too little attention to the exercise of power through justice. Various considerations point to this.

The Cost of the Arms Race

The sheer cost of the arms race illustrates an excessive reliance on power. In 1961, shortly after he retired from the presidency, Dwight D. Eisenhower said at the Naval War College:

. . . We know that the Communists seek to break the economy of the United States—an economy that is based on free enterprise and sound currency. If we, therefore, put one more dollar in a weapons system that we should, we are weakening the defense of the United States.

While more than a sound economy is at stake in military spending, Eisenhower's misgiving was well-placed, because over the years most of the deficit in our federal budgets can be accounted for by heavy defense spending.

122

Military overspend has only one virtue: it creates jobs. But it does so at an exorbitant cost; and, like building pyramids, it constitutes a dead-end use of resources, neither stimulating long-range economic gains nor adding to the quality of life. It results in a substantial increase each year in the amount of the budget that goes for interest rather than for goods and services, thus obligating future federal administrations for immense expenditures over which they have no control.

In 1974 the United States spent $78 billion for defense. In 1975 that figure rose to $85 billion. For 1976 the Administration presented a defense budget of $94 billion. The percentage for defense in the U.S. budget has been declining, but in dollar amounts it has been rapidly on the rise. And if government projections to 1980 hold, the $141 billion for defense that year will represent a growing percentage, as well.

Staggering as the sums spent for the arms race are in themselves, they can best be measured by comparisons:

- Each billion dollars represents 600 additional calories and 20 additional grams of protein that could feed 50 million of the world's undernourished children for a year.
- U.S. spending for defense alone is about seven times the total national budget of India and almost equals India's entire GNP.
- U.S. spending for defense exceeds the total income of the poorest billion people on earth.
- Worldwide, military expenditures are well above $250 billion annually and exceed the total income of the poorer half of the world, with billions of dollars to spare.

Contrasting military spending with the aid given to poor countries, Robert S. McNamara, President of the World Bank, called it "the mark of an ultimate, and I sometimes fear, incurable folly."[1]

The United States devours about $246 million each day for current military purposes—more than the entire annual budget of the UN World Food Program. In 16 hours the U.S. military spends more than the World Health Organization and the Food and Agriculture Organization spend in a year. It takes the Department of Defense a mere 29 hours to consume what the UN Development Program uses in a year. The United States allocates about 70 times more for military defense than it does for economic assistance, if the latter is honestly counted—our assistance to the poor used up in less than a week. U.S. officials excuse our poor record in aid-giving on the basis of our "far heavier share of the common defense burden"—to cite President Nixon's Task Force on International Development. But this is a let-them-eat-missiles policy.

The Administration's 1976 budget for military defense amounts to an average cost of about $1,900 for a family of four, quite apart from interest payments (another $650) or veterans' benefits ($300). In effect that budget asks every man, woman and child in this country to pay the federal government, on average, approximately:

$450 for current military costs
　35 for education
　17 for job training and employment services
　18 for housing
　37 for natural resources and the environment
　6 for economic assistance to hungry nations. (The $6 figure is based on unpadded accounting.)

Stuart Symington, former Secretary of the Air Force and the only U.S. Senator serving on both the Armed Services and the Foreign Relations Committees, has said that we could cut the cost of defense spending by one-fourth or more by withdrawing from half of our major military bases abroad and by eliminating duplications caused by interservice rivalry. According to Robert S. McNamara, Secretary of Defense under Presidents Kennedy and Johnson, "My problem was never to get sufficient money for defense, but, rather, to avoid buying weapons that weren't needed."[2]

At the UN Special Assembly on Raw Materials in April 1974, Secretary of State Henry A. Kissinger said, "The hopes of development will be mocked if resources continue to be consumed by an ever-increasing spiral of armaments." But the mockery continues.

The Military-Industrial Complex

The military-industrial complex has gained too much influence. In his farewell message to Congress, President Eisenhower warned:

> In the councils of government we must guard against the acquisition of unwarranted influence, whether sought or unsought, by the military-industrial complex. The potential for the disastrous rise of misplaced power exists and will persist. We must never let the weight of this combination endanger our liberties or democratic processes. We should never take anything for granted.

The new U.S. experience of an immense military establishment has had a "total influence—economic, political, even spiritual," Eisenhower said, and added that it was felt at every level of government. He sensed no diabolical plot, or even, he implied, an evil intention—for the danger exists whether the influence is "sought or unsought." When the military and industrial sectors serve their acknowledged functions, they automatically exercise an enormous power that generates its own momentum. Few others are knowledgeable enough in military affairs to counterbalance their requests. President Nixon's blue-ribbon Defense Panel concluded that not even the President and the Secretary of Defense had staffs competent to evaluate recommendations of the Joint Chiefs of Staff or field commanders.

A military leader, trained to cope with the threat of attack, must plan for the worst possible contingencies. He must suspect an adversary's motives at all times, and is tempted, by nature of his responsibility, to exaggerate the enemy's capabilities. Unless it is carefully controlled, this process may weaken rather than build the nation's security. McNamara has reflected:

> We, for instance, didn't plan to have the numerical advantage that we had in 1966 or 1967 vis-a-vis the Soviets. We didn't need it. The reason we had it was this range of uncertainty that one must guard against, and there's no other way to guard against it than by, in a sense, assuming the worst and acting accordingly. Then, when the worst doesn't happen, you've got more than you need, and that's bad enough. But worse than that is the fact that they see you have it, and

they react, and then you've got to do it again. And that's exactly what happened. That's what causes escalation; that is what makes it so dangerous.[3]

If military leaders tend to gather undue influence, so do leaders of industry. Like the military, industry finds itself spilling into a forbidden area simply by doing well what it is expected to do. Anxious to develop and sell its wares to a good customer (the U.S. government), industry pushes the arms race by acting toward the government the way it acts toward any other big customer.

The fact that each contract means jobs and taxes in one or more congressional districts gives defense industries considerable leverage. When the issue of the controversial B-1 bomber came before Congress, Rockwell International, its chief contractor, argued that even though the bomber was to be built in California, suppliers and major contractors in 48 states would benefit. "If the B-1 were put into full production more than 69,000 persons would be employed directly on the program and an additional 122,700 jobs would be generated or supported" indirectly, said Rockwell.

The government has been a generous customer. In 1970 the General Accounting Office reported that an analysis of 146 defense contracts showed an average pretax profit on total capital investment of 28.3 percent, or roughly twice the normal average for manufacturing profits. Profiteering encourages contractors to invent military improvements and promote their products—which puts them in the business of trying to influence policy.

The effort, technology, and money that go into war preparations are matched, astonishingly, by almost no preparation for peace. A few years ago Senator Abraham Ribicoff's subcommittee on Executive Reorganization and Governmental Research sent out a questionnaire to 118 major industries, 18 big-city mayors, and seven labor leaders regarding preparations for conversion of industry from wartime to peacetime. Senator Ribicoff summarized the findings this way:

In general, the responses indicated that private industry is not interested in initiating any major attempts at meeting critical public needs. Most industries have no plans or projects designed to apply their resources to civilian problems. Furthermore, they indicated an unwillingness to initiate such actions without a firm commitment from the Government that their efforts will quickly reap the financial rewards to which they are accustomed. Otherwise, they appear eager to pursue greater defense contracts or stick to commercial products within the private sector.[4]

The government freely plans and subsidizes inflationary war preparations, but is afraid to plan and subsidize peace. By defaulting on that responsibility the government makes itself vulnerable to the unwarranted influence of the military-industrial complex.

Nuclear Overkill

We have long ago passed the point of nuclear overkill. In 1974 the United States had 36 strategic nuclear weapons for every Soviet center of 100,000 or more, while the Soviets had 11 such weapons for every U.S. city of 100,000 or more. The Soviets had more nuclear tonnage, however. In addition the United States had 22,000, and the Soviets about 6,000 tactical nuclear weapons.

The 1974 Vladivostok agreement between this country and the Soviet Union limits each side to 2,400 nuclear "delivery vehicles," 1,320 of which can be armed with MIRV's (multiple warheads). The ceiling is so far above current levels that its initial impact has been to accelerate nuclear competition.

"Overkill" is the word that has emerged from this nightmare. Each side has the capability of wiping out its opponents many times over, even if one concedes the destruction of most missiles before they are launched as a result of a first strike by the enemy, and adds to that a generous number of failures. The irony is that either side requires only one thing: enough nuclear retaliatory power to discourage the other from striking first. How much would that be? Probably the mere likelihood that several nuclear warheads would reach their target.

How do we account for the impulses that prompt nations to successively higher and more sophisticated levels of overkill? At root may be the instinct that you have to stay (or get) ahead of the enemy because "more powerful means more safe." Any worthwhile steps toward defusing nuclear antagonism involve hidden risks, but not nearly the risk of continuing an arms race that mires both the United States and the Soviet Union more deeply in nuclear terror, increasing their power and paradoxically decreasing the security of each.

Peddling Arms

The poor nations, too, are engaged in an arms race—and we are their chief supplier. Military spending for them has risen even more rapidly, on a percentage basis, than has that of the rich nations. For 1973 the Pakistani government allocated $405 million for defense from a total national budget of $608 million. By comparison $20 million was marked for a "massive program of low-cost housing and environmental improvement." According to a 1974 report, Egypt is spending $3 billion a year on defense—one-fourth of its national budget—despite growing poverty in that country.

The United States leads all competitors in the lucrative arms market. U.S. sales jumped from $1 billion in 1970 to more than $8 billion in 1974, most of it going to the Middle East. No longer do we sell only cast-offs, but the most advanced weapons. As yet Congress has no control over these cash sales.

A new twist appeared early in 1975 when a U.S. corporation (Vinnell) signed a $77 million contract to train four Saudi Arabian battalions. The Pentagon later announced that private U.S. companies had been increasingly contracted to train military personnel abroad, with U.S. teams then under contracts worth $727 million in 34 countries.

One result of what *Time* magazine calls "this vast and insane flow of weapons" is that we end up selling to nations that fight each other. The argument, "If we don't sell it to them, somebody else will," sounds like the excuse of a drug pusher. The United States should scale down its participation in the poor nations' arms race and instead support peaceful development.

U.S. Military Presence

We have overextended our military presence abroad. The war in Vietnam dramatizes this overextension most vividly, but even apart from Indochina the U.S. military establishment spreads far and wide. In 1969 Defense Secretary Melvin Laird said, "We've had some 15,000 [nuclear] warheads stored all over the world for the last 10 years,"[5] although not even Congress knows where they are. In 1972 the Pentagon put the number of U.S. military bases scattered around the globe (excluding U.S. territory, Thailand, and Vietnam) at 367. This formidable global military presence stands behind the impression that the United States wants to police the world.

Regardless of the justification for garrisoning our troops throughout the world after World War II, these forces should now be sharply reduced. Neither our defense nor the protection of treaty nations requires us to maintain such an extensive network.

U.S. military missions and counterinsurgency efforts abroad provide a less visible but no less offensive presence. This program includes research, training, and equipment for military and police officers, as well as the intelligence network of the CIA. Counterinsurgency is a legitimate domestic concern, especially where there are high levels of social unrest and the possibility of communist exploitation. Unfortunately it has not been possible to keep such U.S. programs from strengthening regressive and undemocratic forces in a number of countries, especially in Latin America.

The military in a free country is one part of the delicate balance between liberty and security. In the United States our tradition of liberty is strong enough so that the military does not present a great danger to freedom. But that is not the case in most nations. The people of Brazil, where the largest U.S. military mission in Latin America has operated, widely blame the United States—rightly or wrongly—for the most repressive features of that country's military dictatorship. It is almost beside the point to argue about the extent to which these U.S. military projects have been misused or misunderstood. It is enough to realize that today they arouse hostility toward our country and in many cases undermine our goals.

Overkill and Underfeed

There are various standpoints from which to assess the U.S. military posture. The one that concerns us here is its impact on hungry people. From that standpoint the assessment is this: Excessive reliance on military power has blurred the nation's vision of its founding ideals and diverted us from leading a global effort to end hunger. This is especially apparent in the contrast between soaring military costs and increasingly marginal development assistance. Overkill and underfeed have walked together.

Less than two months after he became President, Dwight D. Eisenhower said, "Every gun that is made, every warship launched, every rocket fired signifies, in the final sense, a theft from those who hunger and are not fed, those who are cold and are not clothed."[6] A more judicious use of power would help to reverse this "theft from those who hunger" by releasing many billions of dollars each year for peaceful development.

Part IV

A Program for Action

13
A Citizens' Movement

A few years ago Barbara Ward, a devout Christian and a well-known development economist from England, took part in an international conference of church leaders and lay professionals. It was a consultation of the Committee on Society, Development and Peace (jointly established by the Pontifical Commission on Justice and Peace and the World Council of Churches) on the question of Christian responsibility in a world of hunger and poverty. Buoyed by the outcome of the consultation, Miss Ward told a handful of U.S. Senators in Washington that the churches in the United States were about to build broad public support for development in the poor countries.

"I'll call you when I get the first letter," responded Senator Walter Mondale. A few years later he said, "I haven't had to make that call yet."

Why?

Where are the Christians?

Mondale's response underscores a critical "citizenship gap" —failure on the part of ordinary citizens like readers of this book, who *do* care about hungry people, to express that concern on specific issues to those who decide public policy. Because the decision-makers have not heard from us, they have taken our silence to mean indifference or even hostility to U.S. policies that would help hungry people. As a result, the entire nation has moved increasingly away from the poor countries.

Attempting to change that situation is a newly-formed and rapidly growing Christian citizens' movement called Bread for the World (235 East 49th St., New York, N.Y. 10017). Bread for the World enlists members who in turn contact government leaders on policy matters that have a direct bearing on world hunger. It is a movement that holds promise for helping, with others, to turn this nation around on the hunger issue.

The Formation of a Movement

The idea of Bread for the World began when a handful of Christians in New York started to reflect on what the churches were doing—and not doing—about world hunger and poverty. The group concluded that the churches have two great strengths and one critical weakness in this area. The first strength is a solid track record in world relief. The church relief and development agencies, such as Catholic Relief Services, Church World Service, and World Vision, have done outstanding work. Although Christians could and should multiply support for these agencies, millions do contribute generously to them.

Another strength among the churches has been in official pronouncements. Whether issued by individual leaders, or by agencies or denominations, these top-level statements have been remarkably perceptive about hunger and poverty, and about the need for Christians to respond also in their capacity as citizens.

The trouble has been that these pronouncements are almost uniformly ignored. Christians at the parish level have not been mobilized to carry out the policies urged. The difference between the *recommendations* of the Sodepax consultation that Barbara Ward attended and the *actual response* that Walter Mondale knew by experience to expect from church members illustrates this.

The churches have the theology and the resolutions—but not the action—when it comes to the crucial matter of Christians helping to shape public policy relating to hunger.

The New York group wanted to organize, in every congressional district across the land, a nucleus of Christians committed to reaching their members of Congress or other government officials on targeted issues that affect hungry people. They envisioned a "citizens' lobby"—not a lobby of professionals in Washington, but of voters from the grass roots, willing as "folks back home" to advocate the cause of hungry people to their elected representatives.

In the spring of 1973 Bread for the World announced its formation to a small number of people in New York City. Hunger was not in the news. Churches were retrenching on social justice programs. And the organizing committee of seven Protestants and seven Catholics had neither staff nor money. But several hundred responded to an appeal for membership at $10 a year —enough encouragement to prompt groundwork for organizing nationally.

By January 1974 Bread for the World had assembled a Board of Directors that spanned the denominational spectrum: Protestant, Catholic, conservative Evangelical, Episcopal, and (later) Orthodox. Eugene Carson Blake, who had recently retired as General Secretary of the World Council of Churches, became the President, and Thomas J. Gumbleton, Catholic Auxiliary Bishop of Detroit, was elected Vice President. And in May 1974 Bread for the World began to recruit members on a nationwide basis.

Bread for the World's Vision

Bread for the World aims to attract a broad range of faithful Christians. Most are not political activists, but they are committed to Jesus Christ and share his compassion for others. Many sense deeply their shortcomings regarding world hunger. What they need is a tool that will enable them to work more effectively toward long-range remedies for those in need. Our citizenship is that tool.

In order to use this tool we need to sharpen our understanding of hunger and its causes. Listening to the poor, keeping an eye on the hunger situation in various parts of the world, and watching developments at the United Nations and in Washington, D.C. all play important parts in this process. Bread for the World issues a brief monthly newsletter that tries to keep its members up to date on these things. The newsletter also targets specific choices facing Congress or the Administration that require a letter, a wire or a phone call from members.

Because Christ is the source of our life, Bread for the World considers worship an important part of its basis and program. Local groups are encouraged to plan their activities and discuss issues within the context of reflection on the Gospel, prayer and song. Many worthy church-related projects for human justice have withered on the vine because Christians did not see the link between their faith and their projects. Bread for the World wants to celebrate that link.

As the foregoing paragraph indicates, Bread for the World builds not only a network of individual members, but also encourages the formation of local groups, organized primarily along congressional district lines. These groups range from area-wide coordinating committees to neighborhood chapters to parish units. They give the movement a flesh-and-blood vitality that individual memberships alone cannot provide. Local groups can help hungry people in their own localities. They can multiply contacts with government officials on targeted issues through a telephone network, and form coalitions with others in the area to achieve particular goals.

Members themselves do the local organizing. Volunteer "resource persons," prepared through week-end seminars, play a key role. These Resource Persons come from all walks of life, but some of the most effective are people with no previous expertise on the hunger issue or even any organizing experience, who frequently do a better job of enlisting their peers than do the experts.

Membership also provides the financial base of Bread for the World, although small grants from a dozen church agencies have been crucial in getting the movement launched. None of this money goes directly to assist hungry people—for that donors are referred to their own experienced church agencies. All Bread for the World funds go toward building an effective citizens' movement. And, as a movement engaged in influencing legislation and public policy, funds contributed cannot be deducted from a member's income taxes. (A separate but related tax-free corporation may be established for educational purposes only, which foundations and large private donors will be able to support.) Bread for the World tries to use each dollar carefully. Salaries are modest and based primarily on need rather than on position.

Letters Make a Difference

Can messages from ordinary citizens change decisions in Washington? The answer is an emphatic "Yes!" Don't let anyone tell you that members of Congress do not read their mail. They do, and they are influenced by what they read. Rude letters or mimeographed notes may hurt rather than help, of course. But brief, thoughtfully presented points often tip a vote one way or another. Most Congress-persons receive only a handful of letters on any given issue. Often they receive none. They assume that each letter represents hundreds of other voters who don't bother to write. One letter can make a difference, and a dozen letters will make any member of Congress pay unusual attention. Calls, wires or visits can be even more effective. Examples abound.

In 1974 the U.S. House of Representatives unexpectedly—and overwhelmingly—voted against providing this country's share of funds for the International Development Association, the "window" of the World Bank that provides interest-free loans to the poorest countries. Many have no other major source of development capital, and most new IDA funds are now earmarked for increasing food production and improving life among the world's most poverty-stricken rural families. The House defeated the IDA bill 248 to 155. A campaign to salvage the bill not only secured a favorable vote in the Senate, but got the House to reverse itself and pass the measure by a 225 to 140 margin. Contacts from the voters back home made an enormous impact, and although Bread for the World was a small, fledgling organization at the time, it was able to generate a response far out of proportion to its numbers in support of IDA.

In 1975 the House suddenly cut several hundred million dollars that it had previously authorized in development assistance from the foreign aid bill. In this case everything happened in a matter of days. Bread for the World immediately mailed a "quickgram" to each of its members, who helped to secure support from the U.S. Senate for the full amount. Unfortunately much of that was lost again in the House-Senate conference revision, which moved so rapidly that a follow-up campaign in the House was not possible. Still, voter response made a positive impact. One Senator, who had served on the Watergate panel, told Bread for the World through an aide that he had gotten more phone calls and wires on this bill than on the Watergate hearings.

Both of these examples show the futility of making voluntary contributions to world relief, while ignoring public policy decisions. Our neglect of those decisions has wiped out many times over the good effect of all our voluntary contributions combined. The net result is not to alleviate hunger, but to ensure its continual spread.

Does this involve Bread for the World in politics? Not in the sense of advocating one political party above another. The movement's concern is for people who are shorn of basic human needs, and therefore it is big enough to include a wide range of political viewpoints. However, in the sense of influencing decisions made for the nation by Congress or by the Administration, the answer is "Yes." Without taking responsible part in the political process we turn our backs on hungry people.

Resources of Faith

Most Christians perceive the feeding of hungry people as an inescapable expression of faith, and are conditioned to respond. Not enough, no doubt. But they do give to world relief and help in other ways. These Christians can be further challenged with an appeal along this line: "You want to help hungry people, as God has called us to do? Then acts of charity are not enough. We will lose the battle on hunger if we do not change our public policies. Become a voice for the hungry to your member of Congress."

The urgent need is not for churches *as churches* to enter the political fray (although they must take moral stands), but for *Christians as citizens* to exercise their renewed consciences and contact decision-makers. No one need mistake this response as disregard for the separation of church and state.

Our citizenship is clearly our most powerful tool against hunger. Jesus' parable of the talents (Matthew 25) has an important application in this regard. We have heard much about the arrogance of power. This parable speaks about the arrogance of powerlessness—or, more accurately, the arrogance of *pretending* to be powerless, when in fact we can use what the Master has entrusted to us to do his work. The nature of that work is not left in doubt, for the parable is immediately followed by our Lord's description of the final judgment, when seated on the throne he says to the gathered nations, "I was hungry and you fed me" (or "did not feed me"). Consequently the parable speaks directly about the arrogance of pretending to be powerless in the face of hunger. This has been our great failure as U.S. Christians, and it points us to a new sense of responsibility toward the hungry in the exercise of our citizenship for them.

Ironically—in view of Jesus' words in Matthew 25 and elsewhere—it is in their understanding of "last things" that Christians have laid themselves open to the charge of quitting on others, of telling the poor and hungry in effect, "Think about heaven." In the "Peanuts" cartoon rendering of James 2:15-17, Snoopy is shivering in the snow. Two bundled up friends come along, pat him on the head and say, "Be of good cheer!" They walk away, leaving Snoopy shivering in the snow as before, but this time with a question mark over his head. However, the resurrection, far from letting Christians off the hook, gives us the freedom to follow Christ and serve others with hope and fearlessness.

Mark Hatfield, U.S. Senator from Oregon and a director on Bread for the World's board, put the matter this way to fellow Conservative Baptists:

Precisely because all history is consummated in him—because Christ is Lord over all—we must give our lives in his service to the world's need. In so doing, we are proclaiming and giving witness to his love and victory. We may believe that history will end in utter destruction before the New Jerusalem comes into being. But that should not deter us from ministering to the world's suffering and need any more than the knowledge of the eventual death of every person would lead us to abandon any ministry to sickness and disease.[1]

In an apostolic letter on social justice, Pope Paul VI made much the same point:

> Animated by the power of the Spirit of Jesus Christ, the Savior of mankind, and upheld by hope, the Christian involves himself in the building up of the human city, one that is to be peaceful, just and fraternal and acceptable as an offering to God. In fact, "the expectation of a new earth must not weaken but rather stimulate our concern for cultivating this one. . . ."[2]

Many Christians will become citizen advocates for the hungry, if two conditions are met: First, they want to be shown that such a response is crucial for hungry people—an increasingly easy case to make. Second, they must be summoned to such a response by the central events of their faith, chiefly the life, death and resurrection of Jesus. They need to see their baptism as a rising with Christ to a new life in which hungry people have no less place for Christians than they had for Jesus. They need to remember through the feeding of the multitude that to break bread at the Lord's table implies a commitment to enable hungry brothers and sisters to break bread.

Frequently people ask, "The problem of hunger is so complex, so enormous—what reason do we have for hope?" The answer is that Christians do not root their hope in the latest UN projections or some social scientist's analysis of how things may turn out in ten or twenty years. Christians root their hope in God and believe that the future is with his Kingdom, however and whenever it comes. No efforts consistent with this hope are wasted. They are signs of the Kingdom and through them God does his work. The Christian understanding of sinful human nature should spare us from illusions that make so many of today's crusaders tomorrow's cynics. And the Christian hope should give us staying power long after many others have become discouraged or gone on to the next cause.

The Christian orientation of Bread for the World does not give its members a special corner on understanding world hunger. Nor does it deny the deep concern of many others, including Jews, with whom we share the Law and the Prophets.

Bread for the World leaves large and important segments of the U.S. public untouched, so there is a clear need for other and more broadly based citizens' movements on world hunger. Bread for the World's special calling is to invite people from within the churches to take their faith seriously, and, as similar movements emerge, to work closely with them. Some of these are mentioned in the next chapter.

This appeal to faith is part of political realism. In *The Challenge of World Poverty* Gunnar Myrdal has stressed that idealistic motives can be a powerful incentive for change: "When some of my colleagues believe that they are particularly hard-boiled and scientific in excluding from their analysis the fact that people plead to their consciences, I believe that they are simply unrealistic."[3] Realism suggests that in addressing other Christians we appeal to them on the basis of that which claims our deepest loyalty.

Making a Choice

As of now, the nation's leaders usually lag behind the public on the issue of hunger. From 1963 to 1975 contributions to private agencies working abroad increased substantially. During the same period the U.S. government moved in the opposite direction regarding assistance.

An extensive nationwide survey published in late 1973 by the Overseas Development Council revealed that 68 percent of the public favored assistance to poor countries. It was a "soft" figure that yielded to considerable erosion when this preference was ranked with other choices. Nevertheless the survey indicated in various ways that support for assistance is more widespread than is generally assumed. Among those who favored assistance, humanitarian concerns heavily outweighed other considerations, with only 5 percent mentioning national security or communism as factors. Military assistance was the form of aid least favored and most opposed. The survey also showed that when people were provided with fragments of accurate data (such as the percentage of the world's poor who live outside the United States), support for assistance increased sharply.

These and other straws in the wind indicate that the potential for organizing citizens to change the course of the nation on world hunger and poverty is considerable.

What will we do?

Each of us helps to decide how our nation should use its power and wealth in a hungry world. If we choose not to get involved, we are helping to make the kind of decisions that lock people into hunger. Put another way, saying nothing to political leaders *is* saying something to them. We usually get the kind of leadership we ask for on this, and if we ask for none, that is what we can expect.

Few of us, let us hope, want a solution along the lines of "triage" or "lifeboat" (Chapter 3) that would deliberately assign large populations to die. The danger is probably not that we choose this. The danger is that we drift into such a solution by choosing nothing. The carpeting of Asian villages with napalm will, in that case, be judged an innocent pastime by comparison. And we will have fulfilled the prophecy of C.P. Snow that before the end of the century we in the rich countries, surrounded by hundreds of millions of people dying from hunger, will sit in front of our television sets and watch them starve to death, turn off our sets—and do nothing. Instead of reaching out, we will turn inward to protect what we have, as though in a state of siege, said Lord Snow.

But we are not victims of fate. We do not have to let the trends tell us what to do. Despair is unbelief. Ordinary people *can* help the nation reach out to a hungry world. To do so we will have to add to our contributions for world relief the offering of our citizenship.

14
"What Can I Do?"

In the PBS network documentary, "World Hunger—Who Will Survive?", narrator Bill Moyers tells of a friend who, upon learning that the documentary is in process, said, "Bloated bodies! Bloated bodies! Don't show us any more bloated bodies. I know they are there, but what can I do about it?"

What can I do?

The question is often rhetorical, with the answer implied: "Nothing." Because that expresses the feelings of so many, you may first need to advise yourself that ordinary people *can* do something about hunger. Each person has special abilities that are needed. Not to use them is to bury your talent, as did the servant in the parable. To use them is to offer yourself to God and reach out to others. Though individual efforts may be difficult or impossible to measure, they make a difference. They are like the little ripples that in combination add up to big waves.

Second, don't get discouraged. If you throw yourself into the cause with great enthusiasm but give up when you encounter obstacles or when the newness wears off, you won't help much. But if you can stick to the methodical monotonous tasks that have to be done, you can be a mover. Start small, if necessary, but stick to it.

Third, begin now. If you wait for a better time to come along, it probably won't. So start on some things you can begin to do at once. One step leads to another.

Below are lists of things that individuals and groups can do. The lists are sketchy. You can make your own improvements. The suggestions are not all easy, but they are within reach.

What Individuals Can Do

1. *Become a citizen advocate.* Contact your member of Congress (or other appropriate leaders) on key issues. The newsletter of Bread for the World can give you specifics.

2. *Give to your church's relief fund or agency.* Overhead is low and delivery of assistance high. These agencies do immeasurable good and deserve greatly increased support.

3. *Become better informed.* Read books, magazine articles, newspapers. Start clipping and develop a file. Learn about (and from) hungry people in your own area. The better informed you are, the more effective you will be.

4. *Interest others.* Share what you learn, but do so winsomely, in a kind spirit, without anger or self-righteousness, always mindful of your own limitations and the humanity of others—including government leaders.

5. *Discuss the problem of hunger in your family.* It needs to be on the supper agenda. Parents especially can do themselves, their children and others a great favor by putting this front and center in family discussions.

6. *Write a letter to the editor on occasion.* Be brief; pick up on a specific issue, preferably one reported or commented on editorially. Mention your member of Congress, if appropriate—he or she is certain to see it.

7. *Reassess your own pattern of life.* Perhaps you can consume less, waste less, eat, drink, drive or air condition less. Cut down or out the use of fertilizer on your lawn. Fast on occasion and use the money saved for hunger relief. Grow a vegetable garden and share the produce with those in need; or set aside for world relief the value of what you eat.

8. *Help to form a local group.* Groups can be formed within parishes or across denominational lines or in other ways. If one already exists, take part. Push especially response on public issues.

9. *Protect family farmers.* Work for legislation to protect them against encroachments of corporate farming in your state.

10. *Pray.* This belongs first and last. Pray daily for those who do not have enough; for those who lead; for the wisdom to see our own part in the problem; and for grace to take appropriate action.

What Groups Can Do

Most of the items on the previous list apply to groups, and many on this list apply to individuals.

1. *Influence public policy.* Discuss hunger issues. Develop strategy for influencing your member of Congress (or other appropriate leaders) on specific items. Develop a phone network for use when targeted issues arise. Get others in the churches to contact government leaders at the local, state or national level. Arrange a visit with a member of Congress, or invite him or her to a meeting to discuss one or several key issues; but do your homework first. *Always be courteous*, even when you disagree. Do door-to-door canvassing on some key issue to get others to contact an M.C.

2. *Investigate hunger in your area and take steps to help.* For example, who qualify for food stamps but are not in the program? How can they be helped to enroll? Could a "food pantry" for the hungry be set up through the churches? Groups may already be working on local hunger problems. Find them; learn from them; work with them. Take the initiative where needed.

3. *Worship.* Your group needs help. You may also be able to encourage churches to incorporate elements of the hunger issue frequently in their Sunday services or liturgies. Have people donate food at each communion service for a community pantry.

4. *Enlist others.* Contact churches in your area; try to get inter-denominational participation. If you already have that, move the other way and consider setting up committees in each congregation.

5. *Have an offering of letters at church.* Get members to write their member of Congress (or the President, etc.) when some key issue arises and place it in the offering basket. Or provide paper, pens and envelopes on tables, with information.

6. *Form working coalitions with other groups for particular goals.* What groups (grocers, bankers, farmers) might be prepared to back specific legislation, if approached? Or take part in some community-wide educational or fund-raising effort on hunger? CROP might be a useful instrument for the latter.

7. *Sponsor events:* a public forum, a hunger dinner, a hunger hike, a food day, a fast day, a car wash, etc. Involve the youth. And senior citizens.

8. *Make resource materials available at church.* Display books, articles, newsletters, photos, announcements of events.

9. *Sponsor a discussion series or a course on hunger.* The church may (or may not) be the place to do it.

10. *Start a community garden, food canning center.* In some areas these have worked well.

NOTE: It is important for a group, as for an individual, to choose carefully. Don't tackle too much. Do only what you can reasonably expect to do well. Keep your major focus clear, preferably on the public policy side of the issue. Expect discouragements, but don't give up.

REACHING WASHINGTON

By mail/telegram/mailgram:

> Congressperson _____
> U.S. House of Representatives
> Washington, D.C. 20515

> Senator _____
> U.S. Senate
> Washington, D.C. 20510

> President _____
> The White House
> Washington, D.C. 20500

Mailgrams are $2.00 for 100 words, delivered the next day. *Personal opinion message* telegram is $2.00 for 15 words, same day. Call local Western Union office for both.

By phone:

> House or Senate members: 202/224-3121
> White House: 202/456-1414

You can obtain a list of members on key House and Senate committees, as well as a state-by-state roster of the House and Senate, by writing Bread for the World, the Friends Committee on National Legislation, or the Washington office of the United Methodist Church.

For detailed information on Congress and federal agencies: *Congressional Staff Directory*, P.O. Box 62, Mount Vernon, Va. 22121. $18. As good for most purposes: *The Almanac of American Politics*, Gambit, Inc., 53 Beacon St., Boston, Mass. 02108. $6.95 for 1974 edition. Each revision, updated to include a new Congress, comes out *12 months after* the Congress begins.

BOOKS

GENERAL WORKS ON WORLD HUNGER AND POVERTY

Berg, Alan. *The Nutrition Factor: Its Role in National Development.* Washington: Brookings Institution, 1973. Paperback $3.50. Address: 1775 Massachusetts Avenue, N.W., D.C. 20036. Some say it's the best on malnutrition in poor countries.

Berger, Peter. *Pyramids of Sacrifice.* New York: Basic Books, 1975. $10.00. Development seen by a top sociologist.

Borgstrom, Georg. *Focal Points: A Global Food Strategy.* New York: Macmillan, 1973. $8.95. Borgstrom is always worth reading.

Brown, Lester R. with Erik P. Eckholm. *By Bread Alone.* New York: Praeger, 1974. Paperback $3.95. A solid introduction.

Dumont, René and Bernard Rosier. *The Hungry Planet.* New York: Praeger, 1969. $6.95. Still one of the best on agricultural development.

Dunne, George H. *The Right to Development.* New York: Paulist Press, 1974. Paperback $1.65. A Jesuit priest, Dunne formerly headed Sodepax.

Gheddo, Piero. *Why Is the Third World Poor?* Maryknoll, New York: Orbis Books, 1973. Paperback $3.95. Good explanation.

Howe, James W., editor. *U.S. and World Development: Agenda for Action 1975.* Washington: Overseas Development Council, 1975. Address: See organizations. Solid annual overview.

McNamara, Robert S. *Address to the Board of Governors* of the World Bank, September 1973. No charge. Address: 1818 H Street, N.W., Washington, D.C. 20433. Fine synopsis of rural poverty and steps to be taken.

Minear, Larry. *New Hope for the Hungry.* New York: Friendship Press, 1975. Paperback $1.95. Thoughtful response to the World Food Conference with accent on U.S. policy.

Myrdal, Gunnar. *The Challenge of World Poverty.* New York: Random House, 1971. Paperback $2.95. A classic.

Partners in Development: Report of the Commission on International Development, Lester B. Pearson, Chairman. New York: Praeger, 1969. Paperback $2.95. Analysis of the First Development Decade. A standard reference.

Problems of Raw Materials and Development: Declaration and Programs of Action. On the "New International Economic Order." Free, but no bulk orders. Write: Public Inquiries Unit, United Nations, New York, N.Y. 10017.

The World Food Situation and Prospects to 1985. U.S. Department of Agriculture, 1974. No charge. Address: Washington, D.C. 20250.

Ward, Barbara. *The Angry Seventies:* The Second Development Decade: A Call to the Church. Vatican City: Pontifical Commission Justice and Peace, 1970. Paperback $1. Several of the author's books are in paperback. All lucid.

World Food Conference: Note by the Secretary General. Report on the conference. Price to be announced. Order #75II.A.3 Vol. 1, from UN Publications Sales Office, United Nations, New York, N.Y. 10017.

Hunger in the United States

Food Rights Handbook. The Children's Foundation, 1974. $1.50. Questions and answers on U.S. food assistance programs. Address: 1028 Connecticut Ave., N.W., Washington, D.C. 20036.

Kotz, Nick. *Let Them Eat Promises: The Politics of Hunger in America*, 1969. Out of print, but in libraries.

Mayer, Jean, editor, *U.S. Nutritional Policies in the Seventies.* San Francisco: W.H. Freeman, 1973. Paperback $3.95.

National Nutrition Policy Study: Report and Recommendation —VIII, a report by a panel to the Senate Select Committee on Nutrition and Human Needs. $1.55. Government Printing Office, Washington, D.C. 20402.

Poverty in American Democracy. Washington: Campaign for Human Development, U.S. Catholic Conference, 1974. Address: 1312 Massachusetts Ave., N.W., D.C. 20005. $1.50.

Trade

Malmgren, Harald B. *Trade for Development.* Washington: Overseas Development Council, 1971. Paperback $1.00. Address: See organizations.

Population

Rich, William. *Smaller Families through Social and Economic Progress.* Washington: Overseas Development Council, 1973. Paperback $2.00. Address: See organizations.

Multinationals

Barnet, Richard J. and Ronald E. Müller. *Global Reach: The Power of the Multinational Corporations.* New York: Simon and Schuster, 1974. $11.95. The case against.

Multinational Corporations in World Development. UN Department of Economic and Social Affairs, 1973. Paperback $10.00. Address: United Nations Sales Section, UN Plaza, New York, N.Y. 10017.

The Impact of Multinational Corporations on Development and on International Relations. UN Department of Economic and Social Affairs, 1974. Paperback $10.00. Address: same as above.

EDUCATIONAL RESOURCES

Millar, Jayne C. *Focusing on Global Poverty and Development: A Resource Book for Educators.* Washington: Overseas Development Council, 1974. $12.00. Address: See organizations.

THE U.S. FOOD SYSTEM

Hightower, Jim. *Hard Tomatoes, Hard Times.* Cambridge: Schenkman, Paperback, 1973. $5.95. On corporate concentration in agriculture.

Lappé, Francis Moore. *Diet for a Small Planet.* New York: Ballantine, revised edition 1975. Paperback $1.95. A best seller on how to eat low on the food chain and still get plenty of protein.

Lerza, Catherine and Michael Jacobson, editors. *Food for People, Not for Profit.* New York: Ballantine, 1975. Paperback $1.95. A collection of critical essays.

TO THE CHURCH

Byron, William J. *Toward Stewardship: An Interim Ethic of Poverty, Pollution and Power.* New York: Paulist Press, 1975. Paperback $1.65. Rescues the word stewardship.

Kerans, Patrick. *Sinful Social Structures.* New York: Paulist Press, 1974. Paperback $1.45.

Paul VI, Pope, *Development of the Peoples*. March 26, 1967 encyclical. A magnificent document.

Sider, Ronald J., editor. *The Chicago Declaration*. Carol Stream, Illinois: Creation House, 1974. Paperback $2.45. An historic statement on social concern by conservative Evangelicals, with reflections by prominent signers.

The World Council of Churches (475 Riverside Drive, New York, N.Y. 10027) offers numerous materials relating to development. Most denominational headquarters and publishers also have relevant documents.

PERIODICALS

Two are free: UN *Development Forum*, a monthly tabloid that covers development issues with a UN perspective. Write: Center for Economic and Social Information, United Nations, New York, N.Y. 10017. *War on Hunger*, a well-illustrated monthly that reflects State Department thinking. Write: U.S. Agency for International Development, Room 4953, State Department, Washington, D.C. 20523.

Various religious journals treat hunger-related issues with some frequency. Examples of Catholic periodicals: *America, Commonweal*, and *National Catholic Reporter*. Protestant: *Christian Century, Christianity & Crisis, Engage/Social Action, Journal of Current Social Issues, Post-American*, and *The Other Side* (the last two are conservative Evangelical). Christian and Jewish perspective: *Worldview* (170 E. 64 St., NYC 10021), the only one which specializes in international concerns. Denominational magazines provide varying degrees of coverage.

Newsletters or other publications of resource groups listed later in this chapter may be especially useful.

FILMS AND FILMSTRIPS

FILMS: Do not overlook your *public library*, which may have films on hunger, including UNICEF and other UN-related films. *Church relief agencies* (see list of organizations) have good films and filmstrips. Your *denominational film library* can often help. Most films (and filmstrips) fail to probe public policies adequately, if at all. Sometimes the date makes a big difference. Films also tend to deal with one aspect of the issue—a plus or minus, depending on what you want. Agency films will promote the work of the sponsoring agency. A few possibilities, with accent on economy:

FROM WHERE I SIT, 27 min. 1968. Trade policy and development issues. Film Library, U.S. Department of State, Washington, D.C. 20520. Rent free.

HUNGER IN AMERICA, 52 min. b&w or color. 1968. A powerful CBS documentary. $7.50 rental from AFL-CIO, 815 16th Street, N.W., Washington, D.C. 20006

ONE AND A HALF DREAMS, 24 min. color. 1973. Introduces UN programs, showing obstacles to development. UN Development Program, United Nations, New York, N.Y. 10017. Rent free.

RICH MAN, POOR MAN: FOOD, 52 min. color. 1972. Shows problem side of Green Revolution. Time-Life Films, 100 Eisehower Dr., Paramus, N.J. 07652. Rent $55.

THE EDGE OF HOPE. 24 min. color. 1970. Poverty of farm laborers. Maryknoll Library, 25358 Cypress Ave., Hayward, Calif. 94544. Rent free.

BEYOND THE NEXT HARVEST. 28 min. color. 1975. Good brief overview of world hunger with some solutions. Mass Media Ministries, 2116 No. Charles St., Baltimore, Md. 21218. Rent $25.

THE CAPTIVE. 28 min. 1964. Documentary of unemployed man. Powerful. With discussion guide. Can be rented from most denominational film libraries for about $10.

HUNGRY ANGELS. 20 min. color. 1969. Shows effects of malnutrition by contrasting studies of three Central American children. UNICEF. Available in libraries or from Presbyterian Church, U.S. 341 Ponce de Leon Ave., N.E., Atlanta, Ga. 30308. Rent $7.50.

NOT ENOUGH. 30 min. color. 1974. One of the best introductions to development. Poverty in Asia. Produced by OECD, and available from CROP (see organizations) or Presbyterian Church, U.S. (see above). Rent $10.

A PROBLEM OF POWER. 45 min. color. 1970. Poverty and powerlessness in Colombia. An NCC film available from denominational libraries. Rent $15.

SAHEL films and others from relief agencies and CROP.

FILMSTRIPS: Church relief agencies and CROP have good, short, inexpensive, standard filmstrips that can be starters for discussion. Denominational film libraries may help. A few that try to draw wider connections than most:

BREAD FOR THE WORLD. Color. With cassette. 15 minutes. Reflects the approach of this book. Order from Bread for the World (see organizations). Rent free.

GLOBAL CITY. Color. With cassette. In 3 parts, about 20 minutes each. Comprehensive. Institute for the Study of Peace, 3801 W. Pine, St. Louis, Mo. 63108. Rent $15. Sale $50.

HUNGER ON SPACESHIP EARTH. Slides. 1974. AFSC, 15 Rutherford Place, N.Y., N.Y. 10003, and Institute of Social Relations, 300 Broadway, Newark, N.J. 07104. Rent and time to be announced.

GROUPS AND AGENCIES

RELIEF AND DEVELOPMENT AGENCIES

Each denomination has its own agency or fund for receiving contributions. A few of the major denominational agencies, along with several interdenominational or church-related agencies:

Agricultural Missions, 475 Riverside Drive, New York, N.Y. 10027.

American Friends Service Committee, 160 No. 15th St., Philadelphia, Pa. 19102.

Catholic Relief Services, 1011 First Avenue, New York, N.Y. 10022.

Church World Service, 475 Riverside Drive, New York, N.Y. 10027.

CROP, Box 968, Elkhart, Ind. 46514.

Heiffer Project, Inc. P.O. Box 808, Little Rock, Ark. 72203.

Lutheran World Relief, 315 Park Avenue South, New York, N.Y. 10010.

World Council of Churches' Commission on Interchurch Aid, Refugees and World Service. U.S. office: 475 Riverside Drive, New York, N.Y. 10027.

World Vision International, 919 W. Huntington Drive, Monrovia, Calif. 91016.

If you have a community-wide appeal and need an ecumenical approach, CROP is a likely vehicle. It works and shares with Protestant and Catholic agencies.

Outside the church you might consider:

CARE, 660 First Avenue, New York, N.Y. 10016.

Oxfam-America, 302 Columbus Avenue, Boston, Mass. 02116.

U.S. Committee for UNICEF, 331 E. 38th St., New York, N.Y. 10016.

For domestic hunger relief:

NAACP Emergency Relief Fund, 1790 Broadway, New York, N.Y. 10019.

National Council of Negro Women, 815 Second Avenue, New York, N.Y. 10017.

"Citizen Lobbies"

Bread for the World, 235 East 49th St., New York, N.Y. 10017. Monthly newsletter. Membership $10.

Friends Committee on National Legislation, 245 Second St., N.E., Washington, D.C. 20002. Monthly newsletter. Covers a range of issues, with special emphasis on peace and military spending. Membership $10.

Network, 224 D. St., S.E., Washington, D.C. 20005. Staffed by Catholic Sisters, covers many issues well. Monthly newsletter, quarterly, and hunger packet. Memberships $5 and $15.

IMPACT, 110 Maryland Ave., N.E., Washington, D.C. 20002. Action arm of the Washington Interreligious Staff Council. Covers a wide agenda. Sends out background studies, follow-up reports, and action-alerts. Organized by congressional district. Membership $5.

In 1975 groundwork was being laid for the formation of a "global Common Cause" to cover a broad spectrum of international affairs. Membership projected in the $15-20 range.

Research, Information and Organizing Groups

In most instances denominational agencies or task forces on hunger have materials and programs. Among the more prominent are the *American Friends Service Committee* and the *Presbyterian Church, U.S.*, both listed above, and the *Office for Justice and Peace of the U.S. Catholic Conference*, 1312 Massachusetts Avenue, N.W., Washington, D.C. 20005. Two interdenominational efforts of major importance are:

National Council of Churches Task Force on World Hunger, 475 Riverside Drive, New York, N.Y. 10027.

Washington Interreligious Staff Council's Task Force on U.S. Food Policy. Occasional background papers on Congress and food policy. (See IMPACT, above for address.)

Other groups include:

American Freedom From Hunger Foundation, 1100 17th St., N.W., Washington, D.C. 20036. Aims at community action. Membership $25.

Center of Concern, 3700 13th St., N.E., Washington, D.C. 20017. Targets various issues relating to global justice. Primarily a Catholic base. Newsletter and occasional papers.

Overseas Development Council, 1717 Massachusetts Ave., N.W., Washington, D.C. 20036. Respected "think tank," does careful research and produces a stream of inexpensive books and booklets. A basic source of information. $12 membership brings you all new materials for a year.

Partnership in Mission, 1564 Edge Hill Road, Abington, Pa. 19001. Education for model programs combining development concerns with church ministry among evangelical Protestants. Monthly newsletter.

Worldwatch Institute, 1776 Massachusetts Ave., N.W., Washington, D.C. 20036. New "think tank" headed by Lester R. Brown.

On domestic hunger:

The Children's Foundation, 1028 Connecticut Ave., N.W., Washington, D.C. 20036. Child nutrition in U.S. Newsletters: *Feed Kids* $4.50, *WIC* $5.

Community Nutrition Institute, 1910 K Street, N.W., Washington, D.C. 20006. Weekly newsletter $20. Valuable source of information on hunger and local action needed.

Food Research and Action Center, 25 West 43rd St., New York, N.Y. 10036. Primarily legal thrust, but also major source of information on food assistance. Key studies on day care and summer feeding ($2), school breakfast ($2) and food stamp (50¢) programs. Important for local groups.

THE UNITED NATIONS

For general information: UN Information Center, 1028 Connecticut Ave., N.W., Washington, D.C. 20006.

For locating documents: Public Inquiries Unit, Office of Public Information, United Nations, New York, N.Y. 10017.

For buying UN publications: UN Publications Sales Office, New York address.

The New York address is also suitable for most UN-related agencies, including:

UN Conference on Trade and Development (information office)
UN Development Program
UN Food and Agriculture Organization (information office)
UNICEF
World Health Organization

U.S. GOVERNMENT

U.S. Agency for International Development, Department of State, Washington, D.C. 20523.
U.S. Department of Agriculture, Washington, D.C. 20250.
Government Printing Office, Washington, D.C. 20402. Allow about six weeks.

SELECTED BIBLICAL REFERENCES

Genesis 1:29-30 (God gives produce to Adam for food)
Exodus 12 (the Passover)
Exodus 16:1-12 (the manna)
Leviticus 19:10-11 (leave a portion of your harvest for the poor)
Numbers 11:4-20 (people greedy for meat)
Deuteronomy 10:14-19 (The Lord secures justice)
Deuteronomy 24:10-22 (render justice)
1 Kings 17:8-15 (Elijah and the widow's flour and oil)
2 Kings 4:42-44 (feeding the multitude)
Psalm 78:17-31 (they did not believe that God could feed them)
Psalm 146:5-8 (the Lord is just, and feeds the hungry)

Proverbs 21:13 (hear the cries of the poor)
Isaiah 3:13-15 ("Why do you grind the face of the poor?")
Isaiah 25:6-8 (the Kingdom as a feast)
Isaiah 55:1-3 (come to table, without praying)
Isaiah 58:1-10 (the fasting that is pleasing to God)
Isaiah 61:1-3 (good news to the poor)
Isaiah 65:11-14 (the Lord feeds his servants)
Lamentations 2:19-20b (your children faint for hunger)
Lamentations 4:9-10 (happier the victims of the sword than the
    victims of hunger)
Ezekiel 34:20-22 (God will judge between the fat and lean sheep)
Amos 5:21-24 (let justice roll down like waters)
Amos 8:4-7 (the wicked exploit their control and power)
Matthew 5:1-10 (the way to live)
Matthew 5:23-24 (first be reconciled, then offer your gift)
Matthew 6:25-33 (verse 33 is the key)
Matthew 14:15-21 (feeding the multitude)
Matthew 15:32-39 (feeding the multitude)
Matthew 25:14-30 (note the context—the passage that follows)
Matthew 25:31-46 (I was hungry and you fed me)
Matthew 26:20, 26-29 (the Lord's Supper; also Mark 14, Luke
    22, 1 Corinthians 11)
Mark 8:1-9 (feeding the multitude)
Luke 3:9-11 (sharing food and clothes)
Luke 4:16-21 (help for the poor and oppressed)
Luke 6:20-21, 24-25 (blessed are you poor . . . you hungry)
Luke 12:13-21 (the rich fool)
Luke 12:32-48 (to whom much is given is much required)
Luke 16:19-31 (the rich man and Lazarus)
Luke 24:30-35 (known in the breaking of bread)
John 6:1-14 (bread for the world)
John 6:25ff. (the Bread of Life)
Acts 2:42-47 (sharing in the early church)
Acts 4:32 (sharing in the early church)
1 Corinthians 10:14-17 (all are one because partake of one loaf)
1 Corinthians 11:17-33 (selfishness in the Christian assembly)
2 Corinthians 8:9-15 (a question of equality)
2 Corinthians 9:6-15 (he gives freely and frees us to give)
1 Timothy 6:6-19 (be rich in generosity)

James 2:14-17, 26 (faith without works is dead)
1 John 3:17-18 (loving in deed, not just in word)
Revelation 21:1-4 (new heavens and a new earth)

Notes

CHAPTER 1: HUNGER

1. *Time*, November 11, 1974.
2. Moritz Thomsen, *Living Poor* (Seattle: University of Washington Press, 1969), pp. 83-84.

CHAPTER 2: FOOD PRODUCTION

1. Addeke H. Boerma, foreword to *The State of Food and Agriculture 1971*, published by FAO.
2. Patti Hagan, "The Singular Krill," *The New York Times Magazine*, March 9, 1975.
3. Addeke H. Boerma, keynote address to the Second World Food Congress, The Hague, June 16, 1970.

CHAPTER 3: POPULATION

1. Paul R. and Anne H. Ehrlich, "Misconceptions," *The New York Times Magazine*, June 16, 1974.
2. Barry Commoner, *The Closing Circle* (New York: Knopf, 1972), pp. 243-44.
3. "Pragmatic Immorality," *The New York Times*, January 5, 1975.

CHAPTER 4: "HAVES" AND "HAVE NOTS"

1. Peter F. Drucker, *Landmarks of Tomorrow* (New York: Harper & Row, 1959), pp. 160-61.
2. Dennis Bloodworth, *An Eye for the Dragon, Southeast Asia Observed: 1954-1970* (New York: Farrar, Straus & Giroux, 1970), p. 78.
3. Figures for poor countries are rough estimates based on several UN sources available in 1975.
4. Georg A. Borgstrom, "The Dual Challenge of Health and Hunger—A Global Crisis," Population Reference Bureau, January 1970.
5. Lester B. Pearson, "Conflicting Perspectives on the Development Problem: An Introduction," *Journal of International Affairs*, No. 2, 1970, p. 159.
6. *Ibid.*, p. 163.

CHAPTER 5: ENVIRONMENT, RESOURCES AND GROWTH

1. *The New York Times*, June 21, 1970.
2. Paul G. Hoffman, farewell address as Administrator of UN Development Program, October 14, 1971.
3. Barry Commoner, "Motherhood in Stockholm," *Harper's Magazine*, June 1972.

CHAPTER 6: UP FROM HUNGER

1. Paul E. Johnson, address to the Commission on World Hunger of the Lutheran Church—Missouri Synod, September 24, 1970.
2. Interview with Gerald Leach, "Can World Technology Stave Off Mass Famine?" *Chicago Sun-Times*, April 30, 1972.
3. René Dumont and Paul Rosier, *The Hungry Future* (New York: Praeger, 1969), p. 162.

CHAPTER 7: THE REDISCOVERY OF AMERICA

1. Gunnar Myrdal, *Asian Drama: An Inquiry into the Poverty of Nations* (New York: Pantheon, 1968), volume I, pp. 169-70.
2. Cited by J. William Fulbright, *The Arrogance of Power* (New York: Vintage Books, 1966), p. 115.
3. *The New York Times*, April 24, 1971.
4. J. William Fulbright, *The Arrogance of Power*, as cited, p. 85.

CHAPTER 8: HUNGER USA

1. Ernest F. Hollings, *The Case Against Hunger* (New York: Cowles, 1970), p. 22.

CHAPTER 9: TRADE: A HUNGER ISSUE

1. Vernon Duckworth-Barker, *Breakthrough to Tomorrow: The Story of International Co-operation for Development through the United Nations* (New York: United Nations, 1970), pp. 48-49.
2. James P. Grant, *Economic and Business Outlook for the Developing Countries in the 1970's: Trends and Issues* (Washington: Overseas Development Council, 1970), p. 24.
3. *Partners in Development: Report of the Commission on International Development*, Lester B. Pearson, Chairman (New York: Praeger, 1969), p. 45.
4. David Ross, "New Hope for Latin America?" *The New Republic*, November 22, 1969.

5. Editorial, "Nixon and the New, New, New Look of Aid," *The Christian Century*, September 30, 1970.
6. John K. Jessup, *Life*, March 27, 1970.
7. Editorial, "Appointment in Santiago (I): Rough Sledding Ahead," *Journal of Commerce*, March 27, 1972.

CHAPTER 10: THE ROLE OF INVESTMENT ABROAD

1. Gunnar Myrdal, *The Challenge of World Poverty* (New York: Pantheon, 1970), p. 455.

CHAPTER 11: FOREIGN AID: A CASE FOR REFORM

1. James W. Howe, *The "Killing" of U.S. Aid to the Poor Countries* (Washington: Overseas Development Council, 1972), p. 9.

CHAPTER 12: LET THEM EAT MISSILES

1. Robert S. McNamara, in a report to the Board of Governors of the International Bank for Reconstruction and Development, September 21, 1970.
2. Interview by Henry Brandon, "Robert McNamara's New Sense of Mission," *The New York Times Magazine*, November 9, 1969.
3. *Ibid.*
4. Editorial, "Planning for Peace," *The Progressive*, May 1961.
5. Cited by the office of the Assistant Secretary of Defense in a letter to Arthur Simon, May 9, 1972.
6. Address entitled, "The Chance for Peace," before the American Society of Newspaper Editors on April 16, 1953.

CHAPTER 13: A CITIZENS' MOVEMENT

1. Mark O. Hatfield, "World Hunger—The Religious Connection," *Worldview*, October 1974.
2. Pope Paul VI, apostolic letter to Cardinal Maurice Roy, May 14, 1971.
3. Gunnar Myrdal, *The Challenge of World Poverty*, as cited, p. 76.

Appendix

The Right to Food

*A Statement of Policy
(Provisional Draft)
by Bread for the World*

*The Board of Directors of Bread for the World offered
this provisional draft to its membership in March 1975 for
reflection and comment.*

Our response to the hunger crisis springs from God's love for all
people. By creating us and redeeming us through Jesus Christ, he
has given us a love that will not turn aside from those who lack
daily bread. Our own human wholeness no less than theirs is at
stake.

As Christians we affirm the right to food: the right of every
man, woman and child on earth to a nutritionally adequate diet.
This right is grounded in the value God places on human life and
in the belief that "the earth is the Lord's and the fulness
thereof." Because other considerations flow from these, we cannot rest until the fruit of God's earth is shared in a way that
befits his human family.

Today hundreds of millions suffer from acute hunger. Emergency food aid is imperative. For this reason Bread for the
World supports the work of church and other agencies in alle-
viating hunger, and urges increased support for them. However,
the problem is far too massive for private agencies alone. The
resources that governments command must also be used if food
is to reach people in most areas of famine.

But emergency aid is not enough. We need to think in terms
of *long-range strategies* that deal with the *causes* of hunger.

These causes include poverty, illiteracy, lack of health services, technical inadequacy, rapid growth of population, and unemployment, to name some of the more serious. Church relief agencies have increasingly sponsored development projects that address these problems. But again, although there are small models of excellence on the part of those agencies, the extent of hunger makes large-scale government assistance essential.

Hunger is also rooted in privileges that may, in securing wealth for some, perpetuate the poverty of others. Because they reflect sinful human nature and are usually sanctioned by custom and law, these privileges are often the most obstinate causes of hunger. The rich can resist taxes that could generate jobs for the poor. Landless peasants may be forced to work for a few pennies an hour. Tenant farmers are often kept in perpetual debt. The powerful, with privileges to protect can use repression to prevent change.

The problem of privileges for some at the cost of hunger for others applies not only to persons and groups within a country, but also to nations. Because the United States earns more than twice the income of the entire poor world, U.S. Christians need to be especially alert to the possibility that our privileges may come at high cost to others.

The policies of the U.S. government are especially crucial regarding world hunger. Our nation can lead countless persons out of hunger or lock them into despair and death. Citizen impact on U.S. policies is, therefore, our most important tool in the struggle against hunger.

In affirming the right to food, Bread for the World seeks:

1. *An end to hunger in the United States.* It supports:

A. a floor of economic decency under every U.S. citizen through measures such as a minimum income and guaranteed employment;

B. steps to improve existing programs, such as (1) food stamps; (2) school lunches; and (3) nutritional assistance for especially vulnerable persons, along with steps to enroll in these programs all who qualify; and

C. a national nutrition policy that enables every citizen to get an acceptably nutritious diet.

2. *A U.S. food policy committed to world food security and rural development, as proposed by the World Food Conference.*

The United States clearly shoulders a special responsibility regarding global food needs. Our country controls most of the world's grain exports. U.S. commercial farm export earnings *from poor countries alone* jumped from $1.6 billion in 1972 to $6.6 billion in 1974—an increase double the amount of our entire development assistance to those countries. While this happened, U.S. food assistance declined sharply. We now need to respond in a way that reflects the more generous U.S. tradition of two decades following World War II.

The World Food Conference charted the necessary path to world food security under a World Food Council that would co-ordinate both emergency relief efforts and long-range rural development. Bread for the World supports:

A. U.S. participation in a world food reserve program, with reserves under national control;

B. an increase in U.S. food assistance, especially the grant portion, to at least the level of a tithe (10 percent) of this country's food exports, as our share toward the establishment of a grain reserve with an initial world target of 10 million tons;

C. a substantial increase in the amount of food made available to the UN World Food Program and to voluntary agencies for distribution abroad:

D. humanitarian, not political use of food assistance, with assistance channeled through, or in cooperation with, international agencies;

E. a fair return to the U.S. farmer for his production, with curbs against windfall profits and special measures to assist family farmers; and

F. full U.S. participation in the International Fund for Agricultural Development, along with other steps that would promote rural development in the poor countries and, among other things, assure them adequate supplies of fertilizer and energy, and accelerate research relating to food production there.

3. *The reform and expansion of U.S. development assistance.*

The United States currently ranks near the bottom of Development Assistance Committee nations, when assistance is measured as a percentage of GNP. By official (and somewhat exaggerated) figures, U.S. development assistance to poor countries amounts to one-fifth of 1 percent of our GNP. We can do better than that. What is true for the United States is true for all countries: "To whom much has been given, of him will much be required." Further, the *quality* of assistance is crucial. Assistance should deliver self-help opportunities primarily to those living in hunger and poverty, especially the rural poor. It should be aimed at developing self-reliance, not dependency on the part of the recipient nations. And rather than imposing capital-intensive western technologies on those countries, assistance should make possible the development of locally appropriate technologies, usually geared to small-scale, labor-intensive methods. Bread for the World therefore supports:

A. a U.S. contribution, in proportion to our share of the world's income, to the International Fund for Agricultural Development as a major attempt to increase the food production capacity and living standards of impoverished rural families;

B. rapid movement toward the 1-per-cent-of-GNP assistance goal;

C. the "untying" of assistance. Economic strings that put burdens on recipient nations should be cut;

D. honest accounting of U.S. assistance. Loans are counted as grants in aid figures. Either repayments from previous aid loans should be subtracted; or only a percentage of the loans counted, because they are made on below-market terms.

E. channeling of development assistance through international and transnational agencies, where possible, without precluding the expansion of bilateral assistance; and

F. adoption, with other donor and recipient nations, of an internationally agreed set of standards on the basis of which the amount of development assistance would be determined. These standards should include (a) need; (b) evidence that development is occurring among the masses of poor people; (c) willingness of leaders to institute basic reforms, such as land reform, tax reform, and anti-corruption measures, in order to reduce the disparity between rich and poor within a country; (d) de-emphasis on military spending; and (e) efforts to secure human rights.

4. *The separation of development assistance from all forms of military assistance.*

Most U.S. aid is either military assistance or assistance in which U.S. political and military considerations are uppermost. This mixing of humanitarian assistance with military and political aid gives the public an exaggerated impression of real U.S. aid to hungry and poverty-ridden countries. Bread for the World therefore proposes legislation to sever completely the connection between humanitarian development assistance and military and political assistance.

5. *Trade preferences for the poorest countries.*

Trade is not perceived by the public as a "hunger" issue, but trade, even more than aid, vitally affects hungry people. In the past poor countries have been compelled to export their raw materials at bargain prices, and import high-priced manufactured products. The terms of such trade have progressively deteriorated over the past two decades. Recent food, fertilizer and oil price hikes have left the 40 poorest countries, representing a billion people, in a desperate position. For them in particular trade opportunities are more important than ever. Bread for the World therefore supports the following positions, which are partly embodied in the Trade Act of 1974:

A. the lowering of trade barriers such as tariffs and quotas, especially on semi-processed and finished products. It has been estimated that these barriers cost U.S. consumers $10 to $15 billion a year;

B. special trade preferences for the poorest countries. These countries need markets for their products, if they are to work their way out of hunger; and

C. greatly increased planning for economic adjustment, including assistance for adversely affected U.S. workers and industries. Without this, U.S. laborers are made to bear an unfair burden and are increasingly pitted against hungry people.

6. *Reduced military spending*. U.S. Defense spending alone exceeds the total annual income of the poorest billion people on earth, the truly hungry children of God. Our thinking begins with them. During his presidential years Dwight D. Eisenhower said, "Every gun that is made, every warship launched, every rocket fired signifies, in the final sense, a theft from those who hunger and are not fed, those who are cold and are not clothed." Bread for the World supports:

A. greater U.S. initiative in pressing for arms limitation agreements and mutual cutbacks in existing arms as well as greater public access to information surrounding negotiations;

B. curtailment of the sale of arms, if possible by international agreement; and

C. adoption of a U.S. defense budget that would reduce military spending. For example, a 10 percent reduction could provide $9 billion for financing long-range measures against hunger.

7. *Study and appropriate control of multinational corporations, with particular attention to agribusiness*.

Multinationals are playing an increasingly influential global role. They transcend national boundaries and often bring jobs and needed development opportunities to poor countries. But they create empires that are not accountable to host countries and often impose a type of development that reinforces inequalities and, consequently, the problem of hunger, as well. Bread for the World therefore supports:

A. the principle that each country has the right to determine its own path to human and social development, including legitimate control over outside investments;

B. efforts to study and analyze the role of multinational corporations, especially as they relate positively or negatively to the problem of hunger;

C. national and international measures that seek fair means of accountability on the part of such companies; and

D. special examination of the role of corporate farming, with a view toward adequate safeguards for low-income consumers and small family farm holders.

8. *Efforts to deal with the population growth rate.*

Rapid population growth is putting great pressure on the world's food supply and on the capacity of countries to absorb the increase into their economies. Population growth will not be effectively curbed if it is dealt with in isolation, but only if placed in the context of total development needs. For example, hungry people usually have large families, in part because surviving sons provide security in old age. Only where social and economic gains include the poor, and where the rate of infant mortality begins to approximate that of the affluent nations, do people feel secure enough to limit family size. Bread for the World therefore supports:

A. greatly expanded U.S. efforts to enable the poor of the world to work their way out of hunger and poverty;

B. additional U.S. assistance for health programs abroad aimed at reducing infant mortality and increasing health security;

C. additional support for research to develop family planning methods that are dependable, inexpensive, simple, and morally acceptable to all; and

D. efforts to modify our own consumption, which strains the carrying capacity of the earth no less than population increases.

9. *Christian patterns of living.*

The growing scarcity of several key resources—grain, fuel and fertilizer in particular—that directly affect the food supply has prompted many to reassess their habits of consumption. This country, with 6 percent of the world's population, consumes one-third or more of the world's marketed resources. On the average each person in the United States buys about 4.5 times the amount of grain—most of it indirectly as meat and dairy products, along with alcohol and pet food—that persons in poor countries do. There is often no direct connection between our using less and others having more. Nevertheless there are important psychological, symbolic and spiritual values in re-examining our patterns of consumption. Bread for the World invites Christians to:

A. remember that along with changes in habits of consumption we have to change government policies, without which life-style modifications do little more than give us a misleading sense of accomplishment;

B. reconsider our personal spending and consuming, with a view toward living more simply and less materialistically;

C. reconsider a way of life in which billions of dollars are spent annually to make us crave, and in turn spend countless additional billions on products we do not need, and which in fact often harm us—all this while sisters and brothers perish for lack of bread.

These things we seek because we affirm for others a right that we enjoy: the right to food. We seek to extend to all this God-given right in obedience to Christ who has called us to follow him in loving our neighbor as ourselves.

Questions for Group Discussion

The biblical references at the end of chapter 14 may be useful in connection with group discussion.

CHAPTER 1: HUNGER

1. How important is it to sense emotionally the suffering of hungry people? What are some of the pluses and minuses involved?

2. Why have Christians been so relief-oriented, but so reluctant to influence public policy on the hunger issue?

3. Joseph's role in Egypt as the "Secretary of Agriculture" offers an interesting precedent (Genesis 39ff.). What can we learn from this piece of biblical history?

4. What responses does the World Food Conference suggest to us as individuals and as a nation?

CHAPTER 2: FOOD PRODUCTION

1. What bearing does the biblical teaching of stewardship have on the question of food production and distribution? (See, for example, Genesis 1:27 and Matthew 25:14-30.)

2. On Sundays many Christians echo the vision of the prophet Isaiah when they sing: "Heaven and earth are filled with your glory." Can we say this to a person in Tanzania or the Sahel who is slowly wasting away from hunger?

3. In the same setting, how are we to understand the words of Jesus (Matthew 6), "Do not be anxious, saying, 'What shall we eat?' or 'What shall we drink?' . . . But seek first his kingdom

and his justice, and all these things shall be yours as well"?

    4. Discuss some of the topics treated in this chapter.

CHAPTER 3: POPULATION

    1. Has reading this chapter changed your views in any way?

    2. If hunger and poverty play a key role in spurring population growth, why is it that so many U.S. citizens think of birth control programs as the lone answer?

    3. What light does the experience of poor countries shed on this problem?

    4. What do *you* think about the "lifeboat" and "triage" theories?

    5. What biblical teachings address these matters?

CHAPTER 4: "HAVES" AND "HAVE NOTS"

    1. What is the special situation of today's poor countries?

    2. Why is it important for us to understand this?

    3. What place does charity have in our response?

    4. What place does justice have in our response?

CHAPTER 5: ENVIRONMENT, RESOURCES AND GROWTH

    1. This chapter illustrates the danger of grabbing quick, oversimplified answers. What do we do when the evidence is mixed, and good causes conflict?

    2. How do the poor and hungry fit into our thinking in cases like that?

    3. Discuss the relationship between life style and public policy.

    4. What biblical resources can we draw on for our understanding of issues posed in this chapter?

CHAPTER 6: UP FROM HUNGER

1. What impact, good or bad, has the desire of people in poor countries to imitate the West had on development in those countries?

2. What type of development do you think is most human, most in keeping with the justice that reflects God's rule?

3. Would you apply to yourself and to our country the type of development you think is best for others?

4. Can we speak of a "Christian" economic system?

5. Why has agriculture been so neglected in poor countries? If we are urban dwellers, do we have any bias against agriculture that might help to explain this problem?

CHAPTER 7: THE REDISCOVERY OF AMERICA

1. What is the relationship between the U.S. ideals of liberty and justice, and biblical themes of liberty and justice? What are the dangers of confusing the two? Of breaking all connections between the two?

2. How do U.S. ideals relate to the problem of hunger?

3. What biblical examples or insights help us understand how a nation should use its power?

4. As Christians we hold a dual citizenship—in heaven, Paul stressed (Phil. 3:20); but he also used his Roman citizenship effectively (Acts 22:22-29; 25:11-12). What does such dual citizenship mean to us, as we respond to world hunger?

CHAPTER 8: HUNGER USA

1. Why *are* people hungry in the United States?

2. To what extent is the physical separation of most of us from hungry people in our own area a matter of accident, and to what extent is it by deliberate choice?

3. What could you do with others to assist hungry people in your area?

4. Discuss the self-contempt and self-righteousness that so easily afflict the poor and the nonpoor. What does the Gospel have to say about the way we see ourselves and the way we see others?

5. What do we have to offer the hungry? What do they have to offer us?

CHAPTER 9: TRADE: A HUNGER ISSUE

1. Discuss the oil crisis as it might look (a) to people from a Middle Eastern oil-exporting country; (b) to people from a non-oil-producing poor country.

2. To what extent do trade arrangements tend to perpetuate inequalities and therefore hunger?

3. How might trade preferences affect people in the United States?

4. What does this have to do with Christian faith?

CHAPTER 10: THE ROLE OF INVESTMENT ABROAD

1. Is profit-making inescapably at odds with development needs? Or naturally in harmony? What are the implications of our answer(s)?

2. Nationalism is a powerful force. How does it come into play in the matter of international business from the U.S. side of the picture? From the side of the poor countries?

3. How does the biblical teaching of stewardship relate to the question of investment?

CHAPTER 11: FOREIGN AID: A CASE FOR REFORM

1. What has changed since the years of massive assistance following World War II—U.S. generosity or the situation?

2. Discuss the difficulties of being a donor nation; of being a recipient nation.

3. What should assistance seek to accomplish and what should it avoid?

4. Discuss the question of charity and justice in relation to foreign aid.

CHAPTER 12: LET THEM EAT MISSILES

1. Can Christians be realists when dealing with the question of military needs? If so, or if not, what does that mean?

2. Discuss the danger of seeing things from the perspective of a specialist—say, that of a Defense Department official; or of an industrialist; or of a worker in a defense industry. Even if we are none of these, how might our own point of view be heavily slanted one way or another?

3. One danger is that we "leave this up to the experts," another that we jump to oversimplified conclusions. How do we avoid these dangers?

CHAPTER 13: A CITIZENS' MOVEMENT

1. How do you explain the reluctance of Christians to offer their citizenship in helping hungry people?

2. Jesus said, "My kingdom is not of this world." Does that mean this world is not part of his kingdom?

3. Discuss the possibilities of forming a public-policy-oriented group in your congregation, neighborhood or area.

CHAPTER 14: "WHAT CAN I DO?"

1. Discuss what you can do as individuals and as a group.

The Board of Directors
of Bread for the World

Richard J. Neuhaus
Pastor, Church of St. John
the Evangelist, Brooklyn

Mary Jane Patterson
Associate Director, United
Presbyterian Washington Office

Paul S. Rees
Vice President at Large,
World Vision International

Victor G. Reuther
Former Director of International
Affairs, United Auto Workers

Larold K. Schulz
Director, Center of Social Action
United Church of Christ

Doreen F. Tilghman
Associate Secretary for
Administration, United Methodist
Committee on Relief

Mary Luke Tobin, S.L.
Director of Citizen Action,
Church Women United

Anita Wenden
Instructor, Hostos Community
College, Bronx

Frank P. White
Executive Director, Interfaith
Center on Corporate Responsibility.

I want to become a

☐ Member at $10 a year
☐ Contributor (individual or
   church) at_____ $100 a year
   _____$10 a month _____ Other
☐ Send more information

Name _____

Address _____ Zip_____

Phone_____Congressperson_____

bread for the world

235 E. 49th St., NY, NY 10017

A SPECIAL OFFER

**You <u>Help</u> Others
To Understand
By Giving Copies
of**

BREAD *for the* WORLD
to
<u>Friends & Associates</u>

•

<u>IF YOU WILL</u>

send $5, Paulist Press will send you 4 copies (worth $6) to give to others . . .

•

<u>IF YOU WILL</u>

send $10, Paulist Press will send you 9 copies (worth ($13.50) to give to others . . .

•

<u>FILL OUT THIS PAGE</u>
AND SEND US YOUR
INSTRUCTIONS TODAY

A SPECIAL OFFER

SPECIAL ORDER FORM

(Send to)

TO: PAULIST PRESS
400 SETTE DRIVE
PARAMUS, N.J. 07652

FROM: (Print/Type clearly)

_____

Your name

_____

Street Address

_____

City   State   Zip

I want to help by giving others copies of **BREAD FOR THE WORLD** now.

Enclosed find $_____ send me _____ copies immediately.

•

<u>MAIL</u> THIS SPECIAL ORDER
FORM <u>TODAY</u>